FLORIDA TEST PREP
FSA Practice Test Book
English Language Arts
Grade 3

© 2017 by Test Master Press Florida

All rights reserved. No part of this book may be reproduced or transmitted in any form or by any means, electronic, mechanical, photocopying, recording, or otherwise without prior written permission.

ISBN 978-1974005857

CONTENTS

Introduction	**4**
FSA English Language Arts: Practice Test 1	**5**
Session 1	5
Session 2	25
FSA English Language Arts: Practice Test 2	**40**
Session 1	40
Session 2	60
FSA English Language Arts: Practice Test 3	**75**
Session 1	75
Session 2	96
Answer Key	**114**
Practice Test 1: Session 1	115
Practice Test 1: Session 2	118
Practice Test 2: Session 1	120
Practice Test 2: Session 2	123
Practice Test 3: Session 1	125
Practice Test 3: Session 2	128
Listening Passages	**131**
Practice Test 1	131
Practice Test 2	132
Practice Test 3	133

INTRODUCTION
For Parents, Teachers, and Tutors

About the Florida Standards Assessments (FSA)

Students in Florida will be assessed each year by taking a set of tests known as the Florida Standards Assessments (FSA). The FSA English Language Arts test covers reading, language, and listening. This practice test book will prepare students for this test. It contains three complete practice tests that are similar to the real FSA English Language Arts tests.

Types of Tasks on the FSA English Language Arts Test

The FSA English Language Arts test contains three types of tasks. These cover reading, language and editing, and listening.

- Reading - students read a passage and answer questions about it. Around 75% of the test questions cover reading.
- Language and editing - students read a short passage that contains errors and identify how to correct the errors.
- Listening - students listen to a passage and answer questions about it.

This test book contains all three types of tasks. Just like the real test, there is a greater focus on reading than on language and editing or listening. Each practice test in this book ends with two listening tasks. To complete these tasks, students will need to have the passages read to them. The passages are included at the end of the book.

Types of Questions on the FSA English Language Arts Test

The test contains four types of questions. These are multiple choice, multi-select, open response, and hot text.

- Multiple choice - students select the one correct answer from four possible options.
- Multi-select - students select all the correct answers from the possible options.
- Open response - students provide a written answer. Questions may require a short answer of just a few words, a longer answer of one or more paragraphs, or may involve completing a diagram or a web.
- Hot text - students select words, phrases, or sentences to answer a question. Students may be asked to select words or phrases, select sentences in a passage that support an answer, or place items in order.

This test book contains all four types of questions. By completing the practice tests, students will become familiar with all the question types they will encounter on the real FSA English Language Arts test.

Taking the Test

Each practice test in this book contains 70 to 75 questions. This is slightly longer than the actual FSA test, which has from 56 to 60 questions. The additional length ensures that all skills are tested and a wide range of question types are included. Each practice test is divided into two sessions. Students can complete the two sessions on the same day or on different days, but should have a break between sessions. Each session should be completed in 90 minutes.

Florida Standards Assessment

English Language Arts

Practice Test 1

Session 1

Instructions

Read each passage and answer the questions that follow it.

For each multiple-choice question, fill in the circle for the correct answer. For other types of questions, follow the instructions given. Some of the questions require a written answer. Write your answer on the lines provided.

Sarah and Janet

Sarah and her sister Janet were always competing with each other. Sarah always wanted to outdo Janet. Janet always wanted to outdo Sarah.

They liked most of the same things and this often led to fights. If Janet sang a song, Sarah wanted to sing it louder and better. If Sarah learned a new song on the piano, Janet had to learn it too and she would try to perform it better. They both wanted to be the fastest runner and the best volleyball player. They would even compete over who could finish reading a book the fastest. It drove their mother crazy.

"Why can't you girls just get along?" she would ask them time and time again. "I am so tired of hearing your bickering."

They would just shrug and keep on arguing. One day, their mother had an idea to help them get along. She planned to take them shopping at the local mall. The girls were excited about taking a shopping trip.

"Now you can both pick out something," said their mother as she parked the car outside the mall. "But choose carefully because you can each only have one outfit."

When they arrived at the mall, they entered a clothing shop. Soon enough, the girls began fighting over the clothing.

"I want this dress," Sarah stated.

"No, I want that dress," Janet said.

"I'm having it because it'll look better on me," Sarah said.

"It will not! It will look better on me," Janet said.

"Alright," said their mother quietly. "Since you both like the dress so much, you can both have one. But do you want to each pick a different color?"

"I want the blue one," Sarah quickly stated.

"No, you should get the yellow one. It would look so nice on you," Janet replied.

"You just want me to get the yellow one because you want the blue one," Sarah argued. "But I'm not being fooled. I'm getting the blue one and you can choose whatever one you want."

"Fine. Then I'm getting the blue one too."

Their mother sighed and took the two blue dresses up to the counter. She handed both Sarah and Janet their new dress and they all left the store.

The girls looked at each other. They were both confused. Usually their mother would buy them different clothes. She had never bought them the same thing before. They were happy to get what they wanted, but they returned home unsure as to what was happening.

It all became clear the following day. The girls dressed for school in their own rooms and headed downstairs for breakfast. They were shocked to see that they were both wearing the same outfit. They began to argue about who should go and change their clothes.

"Nobody is going to change their clothes," said their mother. "You both chose these clothes, so you can both wear them. Now you can see what your silly arguments have led to."

The girls giggled as they realized what their mother was saying.

1. What does the word <u>bickering</u> mean in the sentence below?

   "I am so tired of hearing your bickering."

   Ⓐ Fighting
   Ⓑ Complaining
   Ⓒ Singing
   Ⓓ Competing

2. Which meaning of the word <u>clear</u> is used in the sentence below?

   It all became clear the following day.

   Ⓐ Able to be seen through
   Ⓑ Fine or nice
   Ⓒ Understood or known
   Ⓓ Sounding pleasant

3. Complete the web with **three** more examples of Sarah and Janet competing with each other.

Playing the piano	running the fastest
Things that Sarah and Janet Compete Over	
singing	Pick out their dress.

8

4 What is the mother's main problem in the passage?

    Ⓐ   Her daughters have too many things.

    Ⓑ   Her daughters need more clothes.

    Ⓒ   Her daughters wear the same outfits.

    Ⓓ   Her daughters are always fighting.

5 Which sentence spoken by the mother best supports your answer to Question 4?

    Ⓐ   "Why can't you girls just get along?"

    Ⓑ   "But choose carefully because you can each only have one outfit."

    Ⓒ   "But do you want to each pick a different color?"

    Ⓓ   "You both chose these clothes, so you can both wear them."

6 Read this sentence from the passage.

> **"Why can't you girls just get along?" she would ask them time and time again.**

What does the phrase "time and time again" suggest?

    Ⓐ   That the mother has asked the question for the last time

    Ⓑ   That the mother asks at the same time each day

    Ⓒ   That the mother has asked the question many times

    Ⓓ   That the mother asked the question once an hour

7 Where would this passage most likely be found?

- Ⓐ In a book of poems
- Ⓑ In a magazine
- Ⓒ In a science textbook
- Ⓓ In a book of short stories

8 What most likely happens next in the passage?

- Ⓐ The girls go shopping again
- Ⓑ The girls go to school looking the same
- Ⓒ The girls put on a different matching outfit
- Ⓓ The girls ask their father for help

9 What happens right after the girls come downstairs for breakfast?

- Ⓐ They see that they are wearing the same thing.
- Ⓑ They begin to argue.
- Ⓒ They start giggling.
- Ⓓ They get dressed for school.

10 If the passage was given another title, which title would best fit?

- Ⓐ Being Your Best
- Ⓑ How to Shop Well
- Ⓒ Fighting Over Nothing
- Ⓓ The Magic Dress

11 Explain why you chose the title in Question 10. In your answer, describe how the title you chose tells the theme. Use information from the passage to support your answer.

I chossed that title becuse the two girls always fight over nothing.

12 Think about how the girls are always competing with each other. Describe **one** way this competing could be good for them.

It can be good for them is they can challenge them selfs.

Summer Lemonade

Lemonade is one of the most popular summer drinks in the United States. It is refreshing and helps you to cool down during the hot summer months. Lemonade is available in most stores and can be purchased as a premade drink. These brands are often made with added sugar and other chemicals. These ingredients often make the drink unhealthy. So we're going to make a healthy homemade lemonade!

To make our own lemonade at home we'll need the right ingredients. You will need 1 cup of sugar, 6 lemons, 1 cup of boiling water, and 4 cups of cold water. You will also need a saucepan and a large pitcher.

Step 1
Start by placing the sugar in a saucepan. Then add the boiling water and heat the mixture gently.

Step 2
Extract the juice from your 6 lemons. You can use a juicer. Or you can squeeze them by hand. Add the lemon juice to the water and sugar mixture.

Step 3
Pour the mixture into a pitcher. Then take your 4 cups of cold water and add these to the pitcher. This will cool the mixture down and make it ready to refrigerate. The amount of cold water that you add will affect the strength of the lemonade. You can add more water if you like it weaker.

Step 4
Refrigerate the mixture for 30 or 40 minutes. Taste your lemonade mixture. If it is too sweet, add a little more lemon juice. If it is too strong, add some more water. If it is too sour, add some more sugar.

Step 5
You are now ready to serve your lemonade. Pour it into a glass with ice and a slice of lemon.

Now that you know how to make lemonade, why not use this new skill to make some money on the weekend? Make a nice big batch of lemonade and start a lemonade stand in your front yard. Here are some tips for setting up a good lemonade stand.

1. Make sure you have a good spot. You're usually not allowed to set up stands in public places like parks, so you'll need to do it in your yard. But it's best if you live in a spot where plenty of people will walk past. If your home is not right, consider asking a friend who lives in a better spot to help you. Then you can set up the stand at your friend's house.

2. Get your stand noticed. You want your stand to be easy to spot. Take the time to paint a colorful banner or to put up signs. You can also add things like streamers and balloons. You could also put signs up at the end of your street. Then people will know that fresh lemonade is just around the corner.

3. Choose the right price. You need to make sure you aren't charging too much for your lemonade. It's also easiest if you don't need to worry about giving change. Set your price to $1, $2, or $3. You should also be willing to do deals. If someone wants to buy more than one, offer them a special deal.

4. You want people to want to drink your lemonade, so make sure you present it nicely. You can add a few lemon wedges to the container to make it look nice and fresh. You can also place lemons around your stand as decorations. You should also cover the table you are using with a nice tablecloth. The nicer your stand looks, the more people will want to buy your product.

5. Add other products. Do you have a friend who makes delicious cupcakes or amazing banana bread? Invite them to join in. You can sell treats to go with your fresh lemonade and make even more money.

13 Read this sentence from the passage.

Lemonade is available in most stores and can be purchased as a premade drink.

What does the word <u>purchased</u> mean?

Ⓐ Made

Ⓑ Found

● Bought

Ⓓ Eaten

14 What would be the best way to improve how the information in paragraph 2 is presented?

Ⓐ Add bullet points

Ⓑ Add a diagram

● Add a chart

Ⓓ Add a graph

15 What is the main purpose of the passage?

● To instruct

Ⓑ To entertain

Ⓒ To inform

Ⓓ To persuade

16 In which step is the sugar first needed? Circle the correct step.

(Step 1)   Step 2   Step 3   Step 4   Step 5

17 As it is used below, which word means the opposite of <u>weaker</u>?

You can add more water if you like it weaker.

Ⓐ Nicer

● B Stronger

Ⓒ Thinner

Ⓓ Colder

18 Complete the diagram by writing **one** of the sentences below in each box.

Add water.   Add lemon juice.   Add sugar.

Problem with the Lemonade   **How to Solve the Problem**

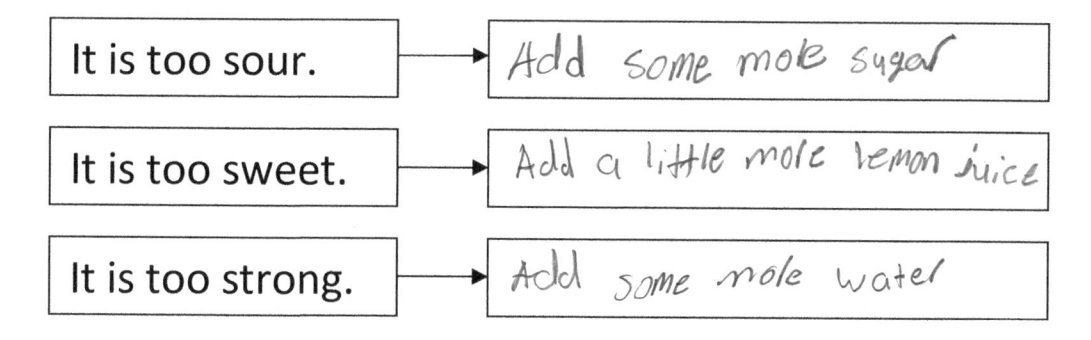

It is too sour.	→	Add some more sugar
It is too sweet.	→	Add a little more lemon juice
It is too strong.	→	Add some more water

19 According to the passage, why is homemade lemonade better than lemonade from a store?

- Ⓐ   It lasts longer.
- **Ⓑ**   It is cheaper.
- Ⓒ   It is better for you.
- Ⓓ   It is easier to make.

20 What is the main purpose of the first paragraph?

- **Ⓐ**   To describe how to make lemonade
- Ⓑ   To encourage people to want to make lemonade
- Ⓒ   To tell what lemonade is made from
- Ⓓ   To explain where to get lemonade from

21 Based on the information in the passage, describe **two** ways asking a friend to help with your lemonade stand would help you.

1: I will ask a friend because he has a better spot.

2: I will ask a friend because at his house a lot of people walk by.

22 Write the name of each item used to make the lemonade in the order they are added.

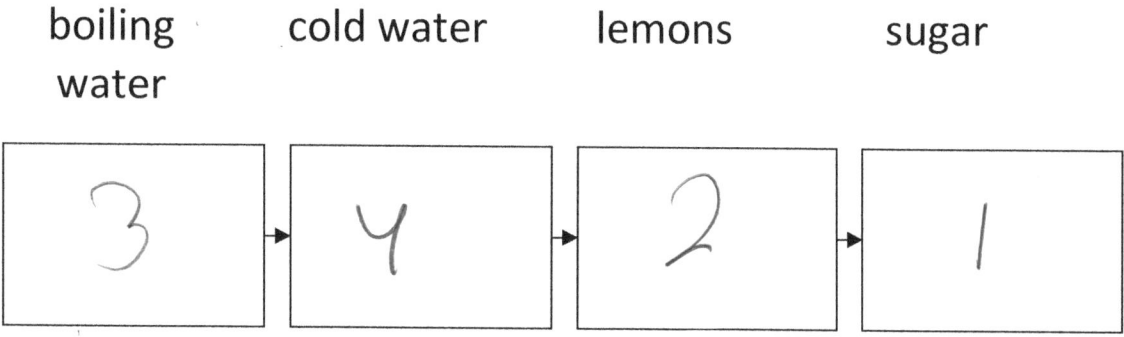

23 Do you feel it would be worth it to set up a lemonade stand? Explain why or why not. Use information from the passage to support your response.

Yes I think it is worth it why because it can hold the cash that people give you it also can hold the lemonade.

A Special Day

Dear Uncle Yuri,

Today was quite an amazing day for me. It was the day that my father returned home from overseas. He had been away from us for over a year. He was chosen to work on a special research project in London. He and his team were working on a new way to make recycled paper products. It would use less water and energy and be better for the environment. Although we were proud of him, we longed for the day when he would wake up under the same roof as us. We had missed him more than words could ever say. Now the day had finally arrived. He had worked hard and it was time for him to return home.

Mom woke us at 6 a.m. to head to the airport. My father's flight was due in at 9:30. "We don't want to be late!" she kept saying as she woke everyone up. She had no need to remind me! I quickly dressed, washed, and made my way downstairs for breakfast. I could not take my eyes off the clock all morning. Time was going so slowly. When the clock struck 8:45, my mom told us all it was time to go. We all raced to the car and made our way quickly to the airport.

We arrived just after 9 and hurried to the terminal to wait. But 9:30 came and went and our father's flight had still not arrived. Another 10 minutes went by, and I started pacing up and down. I kept asking Mom where he was. She just kept smiling and saying he'd be there soon. I searched the crowds of people, hoping to see his familiar face. I stood as tall as I could to try and see every person coming through the gate.

Then suddenly a gap appeared in the crowd and a tall shadow emerged. There was my father standing before me. He dropped his bags to the floor and swept my sister and I up in his arms. "I've missed you so much," he said through tears of joy. We all cried together. I never want my father to ever let me go.

Today was pretty perfect.

Holly

24 Read this sentence from the letter.

> **I could not take my eyes off the clock all morning.**

This sentence shows that Holly was —

Ⓐ worried

Ⓑ excited

Ⓒ bored

Ⓓ patient

25 Why does Holly most likely say that she doesn't need to be reminded not to be late?

Ⓐ She does not care if they are late.

Ⓑ She knows that the plane will be late.

Ⓒ She would never want to be late.

Ⓓ She thinks that they will be late anyway.

26 The second paragraph starts with the sentence "Mom woke us at 6 a.m. to head to the airport." How is the second paragraph mainly organized?

Ⓐ A problem is described and then a solution is given.

Ⓑ Events are described in the order they occur.

Ⓒ Facts are given to support an argument.

Ⓓ A question is asked and then answered.

27 The reader can tell that Holly's father –

- Ⓐ missed his family very much
- Ⓑ wants to go overseas again
- Ⓒ is surprised to be home
- Ⓓ thinks his kids have grown up a lot

28 How does Holly most likely feel while waiting at the airport?

- Ⓐ Surprised
- Ⓑ Anxious
- Ⓒ Calm
- Ⓓ Bored

29 Based on your answer to Question 28, describe **two** details given about Holly that show how she feels while waiting at the airport.

1: _____

_____

2: _____

_____

30 Which sentence from the letter best shows how Holly feels about having her father home?

- Ⓐ *There was my father standing before me.*
- Ⓑ *He dropped his bags to the floor and swept my sister and I up in his arms.*
- Ⓒ *We all cried together.*
- Ⓓ *I never want my father to ever let me go.*

31 Read this sentence from the letter.

We had missed him more than words could ever say.

Which literary device is used in this sentence?

- Ⓐ Imagery, using details to create an image or picture
- Ⓑ Hyperbole, using exaggeration to make a point
- Ⓒ Simile, comparing two items using the words "like" or "as"
- Ⓓ Symbolism, using an object to stand for something else

32 Which sentence from the letter best explains why Holly is looking forward to seeing her father so much?

- Ⓐ *Today was quite an amazing day for me.*
- Ⓑ *He had been away from us for over a year.*
- Ⓒ *My father's flight was due in at 9:30.*
- Ⓓ *Time was going so slowly.*

33 The photograph in the passage mainly helps show that the airport was –

- Ⓐ clean
- Ⓑ loud
- Ⓒ crowded
- Ⓓ cold

34 Read this sentence from the passage.

> **He dropped his bags to the floor and swept my sister and I up in his arms.**

Explain what the father's actions in this sentence show about how he feels.

_____

_____

_____

_____

_____

The passage below contains errors. The words or phrases that are incorrect are underlined. For each word or phrase underlined, answer the question below.

Dear Annie,

I hope you are well. I'm a little worried about how I am going in math class. I can do the geometry quite <u>easy</u>. For some reason, shapes just make <u>cents</u> to me. But a lot of the algebra problems just look like weird strings of numbers and symbols.

As you know, <u>mine</u> brother Kevin is quite a whiz at math. I asked him for some help, <u>and</u> he's not very good at explaining things simply. In fact, he really just confused me even more! Mom is going to ask if Miss Bert will tutor me during lunch <u>tomorow</u>. I really <u>hoping</u> I can figure this out soon. It's getting stressful and I really want to do better.

Bye for now,

Alex

35 Which of these should replace <u>easy</u>?
- Ⓐ easier
- Ⓑ easily
- Ⓒ easiness
- Ⓓ easiest

36 Which of these should replace <u>cents</u>?
- Ⓐ sents
- Ⓑ scents
- Ⓒ sense
- Ⓓ cense

37 Which of these should replace mine?
- Ⓐ I
- Ⓑ I'm
- Ⓒ me
- Ⓓ my

38 Which of these should replace and?
- Ⓐ but
- Ⓑ if
- Ⓒ so
- Ⓓ yet

39 What is the correct way to spell tomorow? Write your answer below.

_____

40 Which of these should replace hoping?
- Ⓐ hope
- Ⓑ hopes
- Ⓒ hoped
- Ⓓ hopeful

END OF SESSION 1

Florida Standards Assessment

English Language Arts

Practice Test 1

Session 2

Instructions

Read each passage and answer the questions that follow it.

For each multiple-choice question, fill in the circle for the correct answer. For other types of questions, follow the instructions given. Some of the questions require a written answer. Write your answer on the lines provided.

No Time to Talk

May 23, 2013

Dear Principal Becker,

I understand that school is meant for learning. It is important to have good reading skills and to be able to solve math problems. But I think school is also important for another reason. It helps people learn to get along with others.

It may seem like lunchtime is not important. After all, I spend most lunchtimes just chatting to my friends. But this activity is more important than it looks.

I am learning how to get along with others. I am learning how to solve problems. I am finding out new things from people, and realizing my mistakes. I am learning how to stand up for myself. I am learning how to say sorry. These are all important skills to learn.

My problem is that the time for lunch and our other breaks keep getting shorter. I know this is happening so we can spend more time in class learning. But please do not forget that we are also learning in our lunchtimes. We are learning people skills. It is important that we have enough time to spend with our friends.

I ask that you consider making our lunch break longer. A little more time spent with friends each day would benefit everybody.

Best,

Simone Anderson

41 Read this sentence from the letter.

> **My problem is that the time for lunch and our other breaks keep getting shorter.**

What does the word <u>shorter</u> mean?

- Ⓐ   Less short
- Ⓑ   The most short
- Ⓒ   More short
- Ⓓ   The least short

42 What does the word <u>benefit</u> mean in the sentence below?

> **A little more time spent with friends each day would benefit everybody.**

- Ⓐ   Change
- Ⓑ   Help
- Ⓒ   Interest
- Ⓓ   Harm

43 According to the letter, what does Simone learn at lunchtime?

- Ⓐ   Math skills
- Ⓑ   Reading skills
- Ⓒ   People skills
- Ⓓ   Drawing skills

44 Why did Simone write the letter?

- Ⓐ To persuade the principal to do something
- Ⓑ To entertain the principal
- Ⓒ To show the principal her writing skills
- Ⓓ To teach the principal how to do something

45 Which sentence best shows the main idea of the letter?

- Ⓐ *I understand that school is meant for learning.*
- Ⓑ *It may seem like lunchtime is not important.*
- Ⓒ *After all, I spend most lunchtimes just chatting to my friends.*
- Ⓓ *It is important that we have enough time to spend with our friends.*

46 What is the paragraph below mostly about?

> **I am learning how to get along with others. I am learning how to solve problems. I am finding out new things from people, and realizing my mistakes. I am learning how to stand up for myself. I am learning how to say sorry. These are all important skills to learn.**

- Ⓐ What Simone learns at lunchtime
- Ⓑ How long lunchtime lasts for
- Ⓒ What skills students should be taught
- Ⓓ What problems Simone has each day

47 Look at the web below.

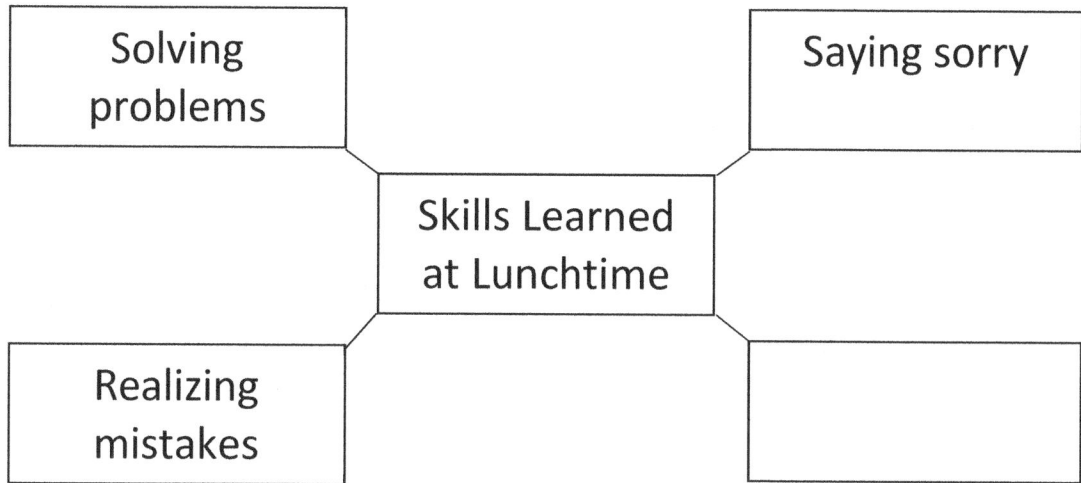

Which of these best completes the web? Write your answer in the web.

| Managing time | Reading well |

| Solving math problems | Standing up for yourself |

48 Which statement is most likely true about Simone?

Ⓐ   She writes a lot of letters to the principal.

Ⓑ   She spends a lot of time in class talking.

Ⓒ   She enjoys spending time with her friends.

Ⓓ   She wishes that her friends were nicer.

49 What are the main benefits of increasing the length of the lunch break? Use information from the passage to support your answer.

The Troublemaker

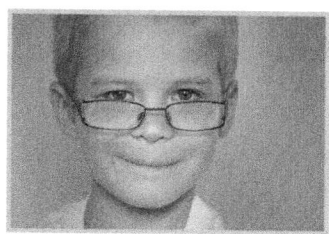

Kevin had always been known for playing tricks. As he got older, his tricks got worse. Over time, everyone began to know Kevin as a troublemaker. Kevin enjoyed all of the attention. He almost felt famous for his tricks.

One day, he was at his friend Jason's house playing hide and seek. Kevin told Jason to hide from the others in his basement. Jason opened the door and started down the steps. Kevin quickly locked the basement door behind him. Kevin put the key into his pocket and skipped away.

Jason called out to his friends. He couldn't hear a reply, so he called out a little louder. He rattled the doorknob hoping it would open. Then he began banging on the door. Jason's friends heard the sound and raced to the door. They called out to let Jason know they would get him out soon. Jason's friend Max pushed on the door as hard as he could. But the door would not budge.

Eventually, Jason's mother heard the noise and came downstairs. She unlocked the door with a spare key and hugged her son as he ran out.

"Who did this?" she asked firmly.

Kevin smiled and put his hand in the air. Jason's mother sighed.

"You seem very proud, Kevin," she said. "But what you don't realize is that being well-known for something isn't always a good thing. Maybe once you were thought of as funny, but now you're just becoming nasty."

Kevin's shoulders slumped.

"I guess so," he whispered. "I just thought it would be funny. I didn't mean to hurt anybody. But I guess nobody is laughing, are they?"

Kevin decided he would have to be more careful about the jokes he chose to play on his friends.

50 Read these sentences from the passage.

> **Jason's friend Max pushed on the door as hard as he could. But the door would not budge.**

What does the word budge mean in the sentence?
- Ⓐ Break
- Ⓑ Bend
- Ⓒ Move
- Ⓓ Listen

51 Circle the **two** words from the passage that have about the same meaning.

friends	famous	tricks
nasty	proud	well-known
funny	rattled	laughing

52 Who is the main character in the passage?
- Ⓐ Kevin
- Ⓑ Jason's mother
- Ⓒ Jason
- Ⓓ Max

53   Read this sentence from the passage.

Kevin put the key into his pocket and skipped away.

What does the word <u>skipped</u> suggest about Kevin?

- Ⓐ   He moved slowly.
- Ⓑ   He was happy.
- Ⓒ   He moved quietly.
- Ⓓ   He was angry.

54   Read the list of the mother's actions in the story. Order the actions from first to last by writing the numbers 1, 2, 3, and 4 on the lines.

___   She asks who locked Jason in the basement.

___   She lets Jason out of the basement.

___   She explains to Kevin why he should not play tricks.

___   She hears a noise coming from the basement.

55   Which word best describes the trick that Kevin plays on Jason?

- Ⓐ   Funny
- Ⓑ   Mean
- Ⓒ   Strange
- Ⓓ   Silly

56 What is the second paragraph mostly about?

    Ⓐ   Why Kevin plays tricks

    Ⓑ   How children should not play in basements

    Ⓒ   A trick that Kevin plays on a friend

    Ⓓ   How a boy learns why he shouldn't play tricks

57 Which word describes how Jason feels while he is locked in the basement?

    Ⓐ   Calm

    Ⓑ   Bored

    Ⓒ   Angry

    Ⓓ   Frightened

58 Choose the **two** sentences from the third paragraph that best support your answer to Question 57. Tick **two** boxes below to show your choices.

☐ Jason called out to his friends.

☐ He couldn't hear a reply, so he called out a little louder.

☐ He rattled the doorknob hoping it would open.

☐ Then he began banging on the door.

☐ Jason's friends heard the sound and raced to the door.

☐ They called out to let Jason know they would get him out soon.

☐ Jason's friend Max pushed on the door as hard as he could.

☐ But the door would not budge.

59 What lesson do you think Kevin learns? Use information from the passage to support your answer.

_____

_____

_____

_____

_____

60 Do you think Kevin will keep playing jokes in the future? Explain why or why not. Use information from the passage to support your answer.

_____

_____

_____

_____

_____

The passage below contains errors. The words or phrases that are incorrect are underlined. For each word or phrase underlined, answer the question below.

The Amazing Amazon

The Amazon River is the <u>secend</u> longest river in the world. Only the Nile River in Africa is longer. The Amazon River has a massive basin of about 3 million square miles. It has the <u>most large</u> basin of any river in the world. In fact, about 20 percent of the <u>worlds</u> total river water is in the Amazon.

The Amazon River is located deep in the rainforests of <u>south america</u>. One of the most <u>intresting</u> things about the river is that there is no point at which the river has a bridge across it. This is because the river flows mainly <u>threw</u> deep rainforests, and there are few towns on the river.

61 Which of these should replace <u>secend</u>?
- Ⓐ secand
- Ⓑ second
- Ⓒ seccend
- Ⓓ seccond

62 Which of these should replace <u>most large</u>?
- Ⓐ larger
- Ⓑ largest
- Ⓒ more large
- Ⓓ most largest

63 Which of these should replace worlds?

    Ⓐ   world's

    Ⓑ   worlds'

    Ⓒ   World's

    Ⓓ   Worlds'

64 What is the correct way to capitalize south america? Write your answer below.

_____

65 What is the correct way to spell intresting? Write your answer below.

_____

66 Which of these should replace threw?

    Ⓐ   thru

    Ⓑ   though

    Ⓒ   thought

    Ⓓ   through

The questions below are answered after listening to a passage. Ask someone to read you the passage "A Tasty Trick" from the back of this book. Then answer the questions below.

Questions for "A Tasty Trick"

67 Read this sentence from the passage.

Now I no longer avoid vegetables.

What does the word <u>avoid</u> mean?
- Ⓐ Dislike a lot
- Ⓑ Stay away from
- Ⓒ Agree to eat
- Ⓓ Identify or notice

68 How does the narrator learn to like vegetables?
- Ⓐ By learning that they are good for you
- Ⓑ By eating only small amounts
- Ⓒ By eating different types
- Ⓓ By eating them without knowing it

69 Which word best describes the narrator's father?
- Ⓐ Fussy
- Ⓑ Clever
- Ⓒ Mean
- Ⓓ Silly

The questions below are answered after listening to a passage. Ask someone to read you the passage "Big Ben" from the back of this book. Then answer the questions below.

Questions for "Big Ben"

70 In which city is Big Ben located?

- Ⓐ London
- Ⓑ Paris
- Ⓒ Dublin
- Ⓓ Athens

71 What is the main purpose of the passage?

- Ⓐ To inform readers about a famous clock
- Ⓑ To persuade readers to visit Big Ben
- Ⓒ To compare Big Ben to other clocks
- Ⓓ To teach readers how to find the clock

72 The author states that the clock "looks down on the city like it is keeping watch on the people." Which literary technique is used in the statement?

- Ⓐ Personification, describing objects as if they have human qualities
- Ⓑ Symbolism, using an object to stand for something else
- Ⓒ Hyperbole, overstating the qualities of something to make a point
- Ⓓ Alliteration, repeating consonant sounds in neighboring words

END OF SESSION 2

Florida Standards Assessment

English Language Arts

Practice Test 2

Session 1

Instructions

Read each passage and answer the questions that follow it.

For each multiple-choice question, fill in the circle for the correct answer. For other types of questions, follow the instructions given. Some of the questions require a written answer. Write your answer on the lines provided.

Roger Federer

Roger Federer is a famous tennis player. He was born in Switzerland in 1981. Some people believe that he is the best tennis player ever. He became the world number one in 2005. He kept this rank for 237 weeks in a row. That is a record! He won 16 Grand Slam titles. That is also a record!

Roger plays well on clay, grass, and hard courts. However, he plays best on grass courts.

Wimbledon is a tennis contest held in Great Britain. Roger has won it six times. In 2008, he tried to win it for the sixth time in a row. He made the final. He was defeated by Spanish player Rafael Nadal. It was a close match. It was tough on both players. It was also great to watch. Some people say that it was the best tennis match ever played. This match also started a long row between the two players.

In 2009, Nadal was having knee problems. He was not well enough to compete in Wimbledon. Federer won that year. In 2010, Nadal beat Roger in the Wimbledon final. The two have competed in eight Grand Slam finals together. Nadal has won six of these.

In 2010, Roger lost his number one ranking. Nadal became world number one. At the start of 2011, Roger was ranked third in the world. He may come back and become number one again. To do this, he will need to beat Nadal.

© Derek Holtham

1 Read this sentence from the passage.

This match also started a long row between the two players.

Which word means about the same as row?

- Ⓐ Game
- Ⓑ Chat
- Ⓒ Fight
- Ⓓ Problem

2 In paragraph 3, what does the word defeated mean?

- Ⓐ Beaten
- Ⓑ Watched
- Ⓒ Surprised
- Ⓓ Hurt

3 Where was Roger Federer born?

- Ⓐ Great Britain
- Ⓑ Switzerland
- Ⓒ Spain
- Ⓓ United States

4 What is the first paragraph mainly about?

- Ⓐ Roger Federer's success
- Ⓑ Roger Federer's family
- Ⓒ Roger Federer's problems
- Ⓓ Roger Federer's childhood

5 Which sentence below is best supported by information in the passage?

- Ⓐ Nadal dislikes playing Roger Federer.
- Ⓑ Nadal became a better player than Roger Federer.
- Ⓒ Nadal looked up to Roger Federer when he was young.
- Ⓓ Nadal plays better on clay than Roger Federer.

6 Choose **two** details from the passage that support your answer to Question 5. Write the details on the lines below.

Supporting Detail 1:

_____

_____

Supporting Detail 2:

_____

_____

7   Circle the details listed below that are facts. Then add **two** more facts from the passage to the list.

Roger Federer is the best tennis player ever.

Roger Federer was born in 1981.

Roger Federer was number one for 237 weeks in a row.

Roger Federer is a great player to watch.

_____

_____

8   Why didn't Nadal compete in Wimbledon in 2009?
- Ⓐ   He was too young.
- Ⓑ   He had knee problems.
- Ⓒ   He wasn't good enough.
- Ⓓ   He had won too many times.

9   How did Roger most likely feel when he lost the 2008 Wimbledon final?
- Ⓐ   Calm
- Ⓑ   Upset
- Ⓒ   Proud
- Ⓓ   Scared

10 Read this sentence from the passage.

   It was a close match.

   In which sentence does the word close mean the same as in the sentence above?

   Ⓐ   Kerry tried to close the door quietly.

   Ⓑ   They had to close off the street for the parade.

   Ⓒ   Joanne and Kendra are close friends.

   Ⓓ   James raced past Jonah and won the close race.

11 The author describes a 2008 Wimbledon final between Rafael Nadal and Roger Federer. Describe **two** reasons this match was important. Use information from the passage to support your answer.

_____

_____

_____

_____

_____

_____

_____

12 How does the author show that Roger Federer is a successful tennis player? Use at least **three** details from the passage in your answer.

A Bold Decision

Steven loved playing for his basketball team. He had been playing basketball for as long as he could remember. Last year, they had won the state finals. This year, they were finding things much harder. There were only three games left in the season. Steven's team needed to win them all if they were going to the state playoffs. It was near the end of the game. They were behind by six points. Steven had just saved a basket with a great block. But he had hurt his knee as he landed.

"Are you okay to play?" asked his coach.

Steven frowned at the pain in his knee.

"I'll be fine," he said.

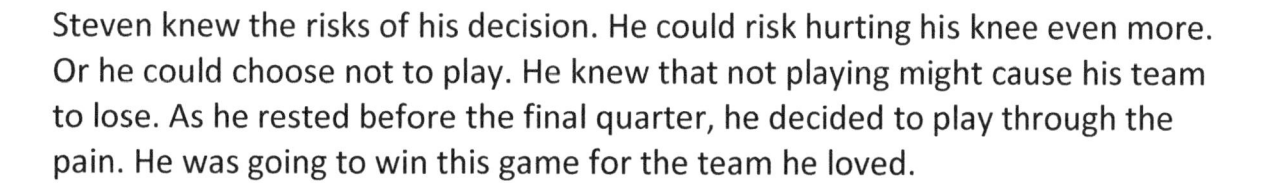

Steven knew the risks of his decision. He could risk hurting his knee even more. Or he could choose not to play. He knew that not playing might cause his team to lose. As he rested before the final quarter, he decided to play through the pain. He was going to win this game for the team he loved.

As the quarter started, he caught the ball after the other team made a mistake. He bounced the ball down the court and threw the ball into the hoop. Steven smiled towards his coach on the sidelines. They were only four points behind now.

Steven kept playing well during the final quarter. He even scored a three point shot from the center of the court. With just two minutes left on the clock, Steven's team was only one point behind. Steven was passed the ball by his teammate. He ignored the pain in his knee and sprinted forward. He headed towards the end of the court. His feet left the ground. He sent his shot into the basket and earned his side two points. The final whistle blew seconds after. Steven's bold decision had won his team the game.

13 In the sentence below, which word could best be used in place of center?

He even scored a three point shot from the center of the court.

- Ⓐ Edge
- Ⓑ Middle
- Ⓒ Back
- Ⓓ Front

14 Circle the **two** words from the passage that have about the same meaning.

finals	games	rested
decision	threw	choice

15 Which pair of sentences from the first paragraph best tell why the game is important to Steven? Tick **one** box below to show your choice.

- ☐ Steven loved playing for his basketball team. He had been playing basketball for as long as he could remember.
- ☐ Last year, they had won the state finals. This year, they were finding things much harder.
- ☐ There were only three games left in the season. Steven's team needed to win them all if they were going to the state playoffs.
- ☐ It was near the end of the game. They were behind by six points.
- ☐ Steven had just saved a basket with a great block. But he had hurt his knee as he landed.

16 What is Steven's bold decision?

- Ⓐ Deciding to play when he is hurt
- Ⓑ Deciding to take the final shot
- Ⓒ Deciding to win the game
- Ⓓ Deciding to try to make a three point shot

17 Read this sentence from the passage.

He ignored the pain in his knee and sprinted forward.

The word sprinted shows that Steven moved –

- Ⓐ quickly
- Ⓑ shakily
- Ⓒ quietly
- Ⓓ slowly

18 Why does Steven decide to play?

- Ⓐ He really wants his team to win.
- Ⓑ He does not want to upset his coach.
- Ⓒ He does not realize that he is hurt.
- Ⓓ He wants everyone to cheer for him.

19   What is the last paragraph mainly about?
   Ⓐ   How Steven's team won the game
   Ⓑ   How Steven felt at the end of the game
   Ⓒ   Why the game was important to Steven
   Ⓓ   How to shoot a basket correctly

20   Based on your answer to Question 19, explain why the last paragraph is important to the main idea of the story.

_____

_____

_____

_____

_____

21   The author would probably describe Steven as –
   Ⓐ   kind
   Ⓑ   clever
   Ⓒ   silly
   Ⓓ   brave

22 Do you think Steven's team would have won if he had not of finished the game? Give at least **two** details from the passage to support your answer.

_____

_____

_____

_____

_____

23 Read this paragraph from the passage.

> **Steven knew the risks of his decision. He could risk hurting his knee even more. Or he could choose not to play. He knew that not playing might cause his team to lose. As he rested before the final quarter, he decided to play through the pain. He was going to win this game for the team he loved.**

What do you learn about Steven from this paragraph?

_____

_____

_____

_____

Rice Crispy Cakes

Rice crispy cakes are popular treats for children. Everybody loves how crunchy they are. The rice crispy and chocolate flavor is always a hit. And they are a perfect treat for sharing with friends. They are quick and easy to make too.

You only need a few simple things to make them. You will need some crispy rice cereal, butter, and a block of milk chocolate. You will also require a small bowl, a medium saucepan, a large saucepan, a baking tray, and patty cake holders.

What to Do

1. Start by pouring the crispy rice cereal into the small bowl.

2. Add 3 to 4 tablespoons of butter. It is a good idea to soften the butter first. Mix everything together with your hands. Just make sure you clean your hands first! You don't want to get dirt or germs through the mix.

3. You should now be able to fill the patty cake holders. Put a clump of the rice cereal mixture into each holder.

4. Next, you need to melt your block of chocolate. Fill a medium saucepan with water. Chop up about 2 ounces of chocolate. Place it in a small saucepan. Place the small saucepan in the medium saucepan. This will allow the hot water to gradually melt the bar of chocolate. Be careful you don't get water in with the chocolate. It will make the chocolate go hard and grainy. When your chocolate has turned to a thick liquid, it is ready to add to your crispy rice mixture.

5. Let the chocolate cool just enough so it does not burn you. Carefully pour a small amount of melted chocolate onto each ball of crispy rice. Make sure that each rice crispy cake is covered.

6. Arrange each crispy cake on the baking tray and place in the oven.

7. Bake them at 350 degrees for about 30 minutes.

8. When they're done baking, take them out of the oven and allow them to cool.

That's it! Your delicious treats are ready to enjoy or share!

****

24 In the sentence below, what does the word <u>gradually</u> most likely mean?

> **This will allow the hot water to gradually melt the bar of chocolate.**

Ⓐ Nicely
Ⓑ Slowly
Ⓒ Firmly
Ⓓ Quickly

25 Read these sentences from the passage.

> **You will need some crispy rice cereal, butter, and a block of milk chocolate. You will also require a small bowl, a medium saucepan, a large saucepan, a baking tray, and patty cake holders.**

What would the author be best to use to give this information more clearly?

Ⓐ Map
Ⓑ List
Ⓒ Diagram
Ⓓ Timeline

26. What is probably the main purpose of softening the butter?
   Ⓐ To make it easier to mix with the cereal
   Ⓑ To help the chocolate melt
   Ⓒ To make the rice crispy cake cook quicker
   Ⓓ To make it easier to measure out

27. What is the main purpose of the passage?
   Ⓐ To teach readers how to do something
   Ⓑ To entertain readers with a story
   Ⓒ To inform readers about crispy rice cereal
   Ⓓ To compare different types of sweets

28. In Step 3, what does the word <u>clump</u> show?
   Ⓐ Only a small amount of mixture should be used.
   Ⓑ The mixture does not have to be a perfect shape.
   Ⓒ The mixture is made of rice crispy cereal.
   Ⓓ The mixture should be a smooth round ball.

29 When are the patty cake holders first needed? Circle the correct step.

Step 1   Step 2   Step 3   Step 4

Step 5   Step 6   Step 7   Step 8

30 Which of these would most help the reader make the rice crispy cakes?
- Ⓐ A picture of a box of cereal
- Ⓑ A list of different types of cereals
- Ⓒ A photograph of a rice crispy cake
- Ⓓ A timeline of the events

31 Which step does the photograph most help the reader complete?
- Ⓐ Step 3
- Ⓑ Step 4
- Ⓒ Step 5
- Ⓓ Step 6

32 What type of passage is "Rice Crispy Cakes"?
- Ⓐ Recipe
- Ⓑ Essay
- Ⓒ Advertisement
- Ⓓ Letter

33 Think about your answer to Question 32. Describe **two** features of the passage that help show what type it is.

Feature 1:

_____

_____

Feature 2:

_____

_____

34 Choose **two** more reasons the author gives to show that rice crispy cakes are a good treat to make. Write the details in the chart below.

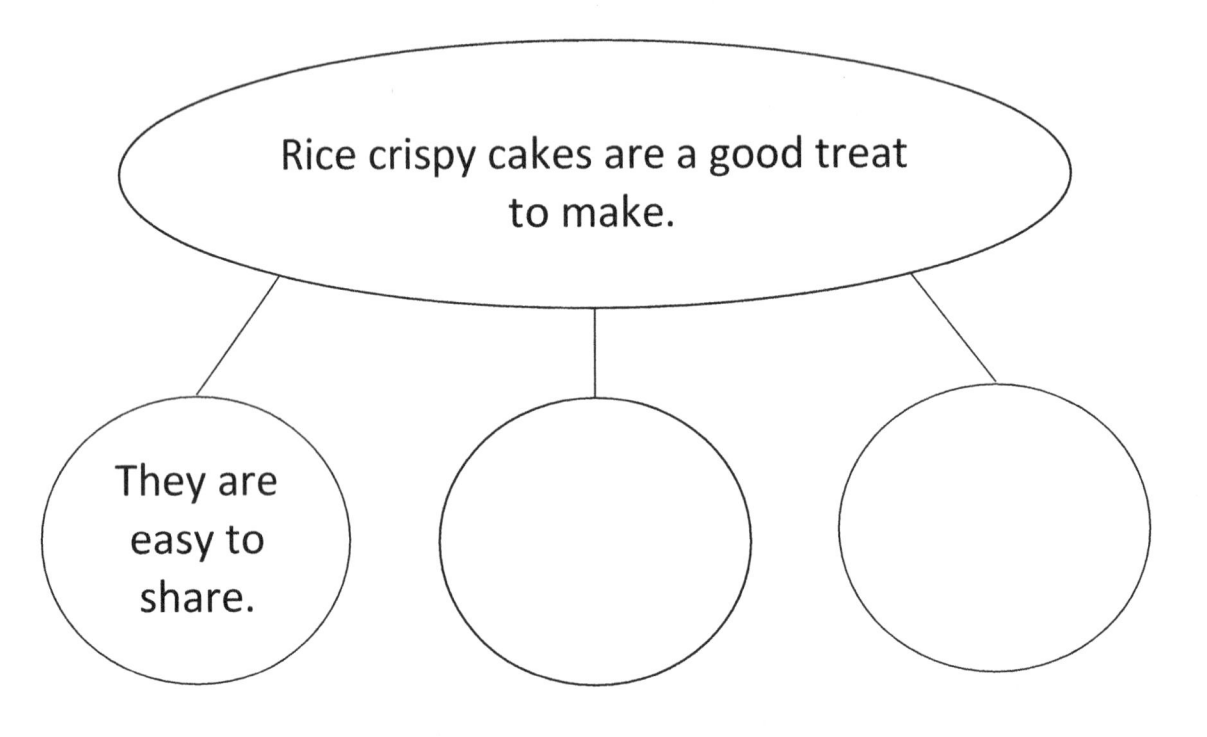

Rice crispy cakes are a good treat to make.

They are easy to share.

35 Choose **three** tasks to be done when making the rice crispy cakes where you would have to be careful. Explain why you have to be careful and what you should do to stop things going wrong. Use information from the passage to support your answer.

The passage below contains errors. The words or phrases that are incorrect are underlined. For each word or phrase underlined, answer the question below.

Not So Simple

The donkey <u>were</u> wandering across the farmstead. All of a sudden, he heard the chirp of a grasshopper. The donkey <u>followwed</u> the sound until he saw the grasshopper. He asked the grasshopper how he made such a wonderful sound. The grasshopper explained that he lived off the dew.

The donkey <u>eated</u> nothing but dew for weeks. He still didn't sound anything like the grasshopper. He was also starting to feel very ill. He started chewing on some grass <u>too</u> get his energy back.

<u>"I guess it's not that simple" said the donkey.</u>

36 Which of these should replace <u>were</u>?

- Ⓐ are
- Ⓑ does
- Ⓒ is
- Ⓓ was

37 Which of these should replace <u>followwed</u>?

- Ⓐ folowed
- Ⓑ folowwed
- Ⓒ followed
- Ⓓ folloowed

38 Which of these should replace eated?

- Ⓐ ate
- Ⓑ ated
- Ⓒ eat
- Ⓓ eaten

39 Which of these should replace too?

- Ⓐ to
- Ⓑ tow
- Ⓒ two
- Ⓓ toe

40 Write the sentence correctly by adding a comma. Write the correct sentence below.

_____

END OF SESSION 1

Florida Standards Assessment

English Language Arts

Practice Test 2

Session 2

Instructions

Read each passage and answer the questions that follow it.

For each multiple-choice question, fill in the circle for the correct answer. For other types of questions, follow the instructions given. Some of the questions require a written answer. Write your answer on the lines provided.

The Bumble Bee

Yellow and black with a set of tiny wings,
I busily buzz around the land,
And boast a mighty sting!

I do not care for fame or money,
I do not wish to harm,
I just live for making honey!

This beekeeper holds up honeycomb that has been made in the hive. The honey is extracted, or taken out, from the honeycomb. Bees can sting, so this beekeeper wears a special bee suit to keep him safe. Bees usually only sting when they are afraid of something. The best way to be safe from bees is simply to leave them alone!

41 According to the poem, what does the bee enjoy most?

- Ⓐ Being famous
- Ⓑ Being rich
- Ⓒ Making honey
- Ⓓ Stinging people

42 Read this line from the poem.

I busily buzz around the land,

Which literary device is used in this line?

- Ⓐ Alliteration
- Ⓑ Simile
- Ⓒ Metaphor
- Ⓓ Imagery

43 What is the rhyme pattern of each stanza of the poem?

- Ⓐ Every line rhymes.
- Ⓑ The first and second lines rhyme.
- Ⓒ The first and last lines rhyme.
- Ⓓ None of the lines rhyme.

44 Onomatopoeia is when a word sounds like what it describes. Which word from the poem is an example of onomatopoeia?

- Ⓐ *black*
- Ⓑ *wings*
- Ⓒ *buzz*
- Ⓓ *sting*

45 In the line below, what does the word <u>mighty</u> mean?

And boast a mighty sting!

- Ⓐ Scary
- Ⓑ Strange
- Ⓒ Naughty
- Ⓓ Great

46 Which sentence from the caption best supports the idea that bees do not wish to harm?

- Ⓐ *This beekeeper holds up honeycomb that has been made in the hive.*
- Ⓑ *The honey is extracted, or taken out, from the honeycomb.*
- Ⓒ *Bees can sting, so this beekeeper wears a special bee suit to keep him safe.*
- Ⓓ *Bees usually only sting when they are afraid of something.*

47 What does the photograph help readers understand? Explain your answer.

_____

_____

_____

_____

_____

_____

48 Complete the diagram below by listing **three** facts the author gives about bees.

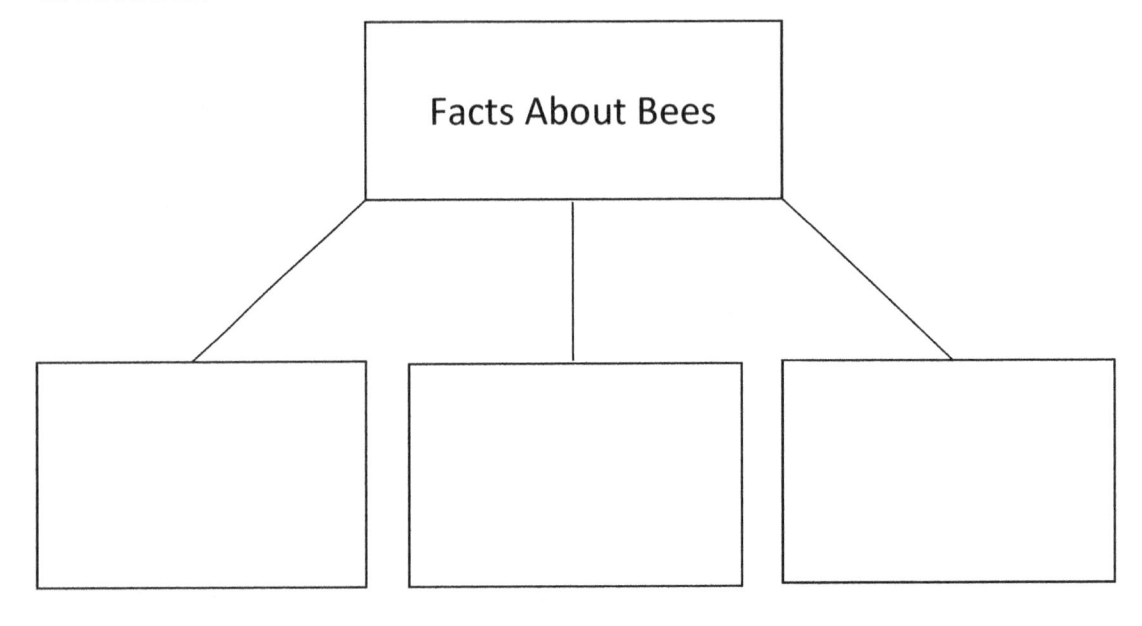

```
         ┌─────────────────┐
         │ Facts About Bees│
         └─────────────────┘
        /         |         \
   ┌───────┐  ┌───────┐  ┌───────┐
   │       │  │       │  │       │
   └───────┘  └───────┘  └───────┘
```

49 The poem is written from the point of view of a bee. How does this point of view affect the poem? In your answer, explain whether or not it helps readers take the poem seriously. Use details from the poem to support your answer.

A Letter to My Favorite Author

July 1, 2013

Dear Simeon,

I am writing to tell you what a huge fan I am of your work. I have enjoyed your books since I was eight years old. I read a story in the newspaper that said you were ill. It made me feel sad. I wanted to write just to tell you how much I like your work. And that I hope you feel better soon too!

My love for your work began with your first book. *The Singing Swordfish* was so well-written. The pictures also helped to bring your words to life. I laughed so hard I cried the first time I read the book! From then on, I was hooked on your every word. I cannot imagine a better children's author existing anywhere else in the world. If there is one, I would certainly like to know about them too! If I had to choose which of your books was my favorite, it would be *The Shining Light*. That story was such an adventure from start to finish. Your book *Rainy Day* is also a favorite. It made me think a lot. And of course, I love *Just Lazing Around* as well. It always makes me laugh.

I hope that you feel better soon. You have given so much joy to so many people. Take care and thank you for all of the memories and moments of joy that you have given me.

Yours sincerely,

Kyle Harper

50   Read this sentence from the letter.

From then on, I was hooked on your every word.

What does the phrase "hooked on" mean?

Ⓐ   Very keen on

Ⓑ   Confused by

Ⓒ   Bent

Ⓓ   Owned

51   Read this sentence from the letter.

I cannot imagine a better children's author existing anywhere else in the world.

Which word means about the same as existing?

Ⓐ   Living

Ⓑ   Writing

Ⓒ   Working

Ⓓ   Thinking

52 According to the letter, why does Kyle decide to write to Simeon?

- Ⓐ He is asked to by his mother.
- Ⓑ He wants to be sent a free book.
- Ⓒ He wants her to write another book.
- Ⓓ He reads that she is ill.

53 Based on your answer to Question 52, choose **two** sentences from the first paragraph that support your answer. Circle the **two** sentences below. Then explain why you chose those sentences.

> I am writing to tell you what a huge fan I am of your work. I have enjoyed your books since I was eight years old. I read a story in the newspaper that said you were ill. It made me feel sad. I wanted to write just to tell you how much I like your work. And that I hope you feel better soon too!

_____

_____

_____

_____

_____

54 Complete the chart by writing **one** book from the list below in each space.

The Singing Swordfish   *The Shining Light*
Rainy Day   *Just Lazing Around*

Favorite Book:	
First Book Read:	

55 The reader can tell that Kyle —

Ⓐ no longer reads Simeon's books

Ⓑ wants to be a writer someday

Ⓒ has read many of Simeon's books

Ⓓ started reading because he was ill

56 What is the first paragraph mainly about?

Ⓐ Why Kyle is writing to Simeon

Ⓑ When Kyle started reading Simeon's books

Ⓒ Which book of Simeon's is Kyle's favorite

Ⓓ How Kyle reads the newspaper

57 Which part of the letter tells who wrote the letter?

- Ⓐ Date
- Ⓑ Greeting
- Ⓒ Closing
- Ⓓ Body

58 Describe **two** reasons that Kyle liked the book *The Singing Swordfish*.

1: _____

2: _____

59 Do you think Simeon would feel good after reading the letter? Explain why or why not.

_____
_____
_____
_____
_____

The passage below contains errors. The words or phrases that are incorrect are underlined. For each word or phrase underlined, answer the question below.

a day of learning

It's a Saturday and that means no school. I decided to feed my brain for the day. This morning I <u>did start</u> reading through an encyclopedia. They <u>will have</u> always amazed me with how much information is in them. I enjoyed reading about Scotland, badgers, and a writer named Aldous Huxley. I also read all about the first President of the United States, George Washington. It might sound like a <u>boreing</u> day to some people, <u>so</u> I actually had a great time! I learned a lot of new things and I want to learn even <u>moor</u>.

60 What is the correct way to capitalize the title? Write your answer below.

_____

61 Which of these should replace <u>did start</u>?
- Ⓐ start
- Ⓑ starts
- Ⓒ started
- Ⓓ starting

62 Which of these should replace will have?

Ⓐ　had

Ⓑ　have

Ⓒ　did have

Ⓓ　will have

63 Which of these should replace boreing?

Ⓐ　boring

Ⓑ　borring

Ⓒ　booring

Ⓓ　boorring

64 Which of these should replace so?

Ⓐ　and

Ⓑ　but

Ⓒ　if

Ⓓ　then

65 As it is used in the sentence, what is the correct spelling of moor? Write your answer below.

_____

The questions below are answered after listening to a passage. Ask someone to read you the passage "The Astronomer" from the back of this book. Then answer the questions below.

Questions for "The Astronomer"

66 The main theme of the passage is about –

Ⓐ   having an interesting hobby

Ⓑ   not being afraid to ask for help

Ⓒ   being careful at all times

Ⓓ   not focusing too much on one thing

67 The astronomer falls down the well mainly because he is –

Ⓐ   not looking where he is going

Ⓑ   rushing too much

Ⓒ   walking around at night

Ⓓ   wondering what is in the well

68 What is the main purpose of the friend's dialogue below?

"Old friend, in striving to see into the heavens, you don't manage to see what is on the earth," the friend said.

Ⓐ   To show that the astronomer has changed

Ⓑ   To show how passionate the astronomer is

Ⓒ   To show that the story has a happy ending

Ⓓ   To show the moral lesson of the story

The questions below are answered after listening to a passage. Ask someone to read you the passage "View from the Moon" from the back of this book. Then answer the questions below.

Questions for "View from the Moon"

69 According to the passage, which of these can be seen from the Moon?

- Ⓐ Cities
- Ⓑ Motorways
- Ⓒ Crops
- Ⓓ Oceans

70 What is the most likely reason the Great Wall of China cannot be seen from the Moon?

- Ⓐ The Moon is too far away.
- Ⓑ The Moon is too dark.
- Ⓒ The Great Wall of China is too white.
- Ⓓ The Great Wall of China is in Asia.

END OF SESSION 2

Florida Standards Assessment

English Language Arts

Practice Test 3

Session 1

Instructions

Read each passage and answer the questions that follow it.

For each multiple-choice question, fill in the circle for the correct answer. For other types of questions, follow the instructions given. Some of the questions require a written answer. Write your answer on the lines provided.

The New York Times

The New York Times is an American newspaper. It was founded in New York. It was first printed in 1851. The first issue cost just 1 cent to buy. It is printed each day. Each issue is read by around one million people. The newspaper has won over 110 Pulitzer Prizes. A Pulitzer Prize is an award given for excellent reporting. This is more than any other newspaper or magazine.

The New York Times is the largest local newspaper in the United States. It is also the third largest newspaper overall. Only *The Wall Street Journal* and *USA Today* are read by more people.

Even though it is still popular, it sells fewer copies today than in the past. In 1990, it was read by over a million people. By 2010, it was being read by less than a million people. This change has occurred for most printed newspapers. The main reason is that people can read the news on the Internet for free.

The newspaper's motto is "All the News That's Fit to Print." This appears printed in the top corner of the front page.

The newspaper has many different sections. It covers news, business, and science. It also covers sport, home, and fashion. It has sections for travel, food, art, and movies. It is also known for its difficult crossword puzzles.

In 2011, each issue sold for $2. However, the Sunday issue is larger. It is sold for $5.

Hundreds of people work to create *The New York Times* every day.

1 Read this sentence from the passage.

It was founded in New York.

What does the word <u>founded</u> mean in the sentence?

Ⓐ Sold

Ⓑ Discovered

Ⓒ Started

Ⓓ Lost

2 Read this sentence from the passage.

The newspaper's motto is "All the News That's Fit to Print."

As it is used in this sentence, what does <u>fit</u> mean?

Ⓐ Ready

Ⓑ Healthy

Ⓒ Right

Ⓓ Known

3 According to the passage, how is *The Wall Street Journal* different from *The New York Times*?

- Ⓐ It is read by more people.
- Ⓑ It has won more awards.
- Ⓒ It costs less to buy.
- Ⓓ It has fewer sections.

4 According to the passage, why are fewer copies of *The New York Times* sold today than in the past?

- Ⓐ It costs too much.
- Ⓑ People read the news online.
- Ⓒ People buy other newspapers instead.
- Ⓓ It has too many sections.

5 Which word best describes the tone of the passage?

- Ⓐ Gloomy
- Ⓑ Serious
- Ⓒ Lively
- Ⓓ Hopeful

6 Which detail best shows that *The New York Times* is successful?

- Ⓐ It is printed seven days a week.
- Ⓑ Its price has increased to $2.
- Ⓒ It has a motto.
- Ⓓ It has won over 110 Pulitzer Prizes.

7 Use details from the passage to complete the web below.

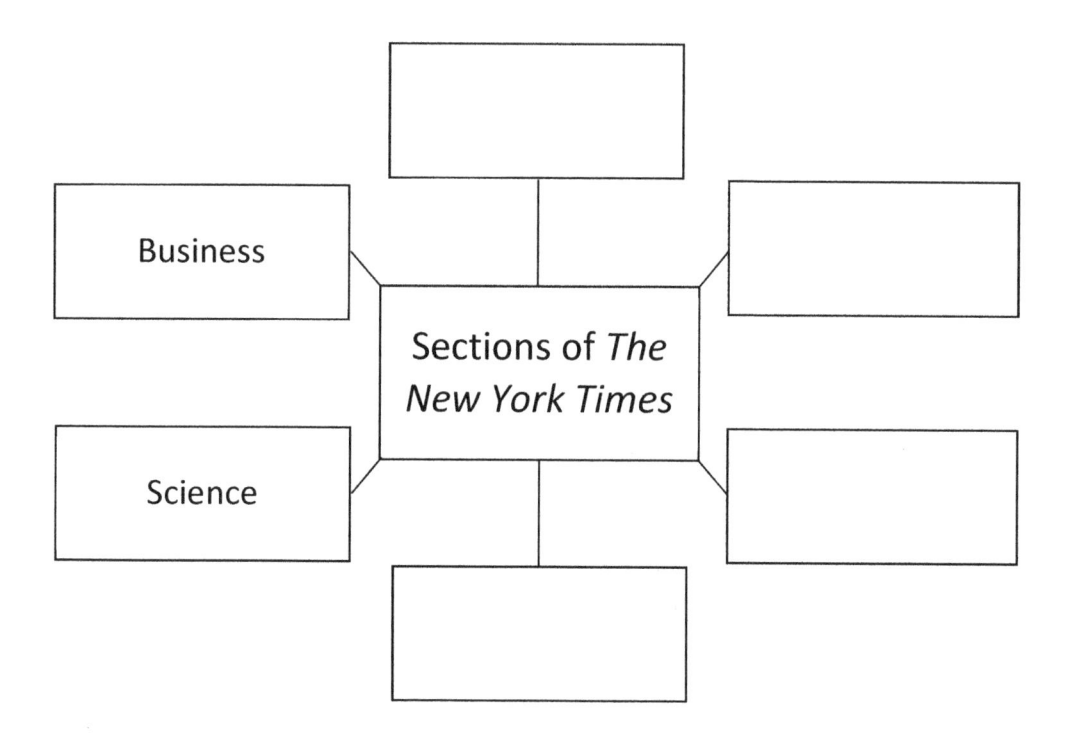

Sections of *The New York Times*
- Business
- Science
- [ ]
- [ ]
- [ ]
- [ ]

8 Read this sentence from the passage.

> **The main reason is that people can read the news on the Internet for free.**

In which sentence does <u>free</u> mean the same as in the sentence above?

- Ⓐ   Jorja gave the kitten away for <u>free</u>.
- Ⓑ   Andy was happy to have the whole day <u>free</u>.
- Ⓒ   The diner was so busy that only one table was <u>free</u>.
- Ⓓ   The beach always made Kyle feel relaxed and <u>free</u>.

9 Read this sentence from the passage.

> **The newspaper has won over 110 Pulitzer Prizes. A Pulitzer Prize is an award given for excellent reporting.**

Explain why the second sentence is important. In your answer, explain what the second sentence tells you about *The New York Times*.

_____

_____

_____

_____

_____

10 Describe **two** things about *The New York Times* that have changed since it was first printed.

1: _____

_____

2: _____

_____

11 Which details from the passage did you find most interesting? Explain why you found those details interesting. Use details from the passage in your answer.

_____

_____

_____

_____

_____

Little Things
by Ebenezer Cobham Brewer

Little drops of water,
Little grains of sand,
Make the mighty ocean
And the pleasant land.

Thus the little minutes,
Humble though they be,
Make the mighty ages
Of eternity.

This canyon in Arizona is a popular place for tourists and adventure-seekers. People love to admire the view, take photographs, or raft along the Colorado River. It took millions of years for the canyon to form. As water flowed over the land, it wore away the rock little by little. Today, the result is a canyon that is thousands of feet deep.

12   In the lines below, what does the word <u>eternity</u> most likely mean?

   Make the mighty ages
   Of eternity.

   Ⓐ   Time
   Ⓑ   Forever
   Ⓒ   Earth
   Ⓓ   Everything

13   Read this line from the poem.

   Make the mighty ocean

   The word <u>mighty</u> suggests that the ocean is –

   Ⓐ   strange
   Ⓑ   scary
   Ⓒ   powerful
   Ⓓ   small

14   How many stanzas does the poem have? Circle the correct answer.

   1   2   3   4   5   6   7   8

15 Which literary technique does the author use in the line below?

Make the mighty ages

- Ⓐ Alliteration
- Ⓑ Simile
- Ⓒ Metaphor
- Ⓓ Flashback

16 What is the rhyme pattern of each stanza of the poem?

- Ⓐ All the lines rhyme with each other.
- Ⓑ There are two pairs of rhyming lines.
- Ⓒ The second and fourth lines rhyme.
- Ⓓ None of the lines rhyme.

17 What are the lines below mainly about?

**Thus the little minutes,
Humble though they be,
Make the mighty ages
Of eternity.**

- Ⓐ Nature
- Ⓑ Earth
- Ⓒ Time
- Ⓓ Sleep

18 What is the main idea of the poem?

Ⓐ Little things can form great things.

Ⓑ Everything is always changing.

Ⓒ Life could not survive without water.

Ⓓ Time can go fast or slow.

19 Circle **all** the words that are repeated in the poem.

little   drops   mighty

water   sand   minutes

20 Explain how water, sand, and minutes are similar in the poem. Use details from the poem to support your answer.

_____

_____

_____

_____

_____

21 Look at the picture of the canyon and read the caption. What idea does this show that is also a main idea in the poem?

_____

_____

_____

_____

_____

22 Based on your answer to Question 21, choose **two** details given in the caption that best show the main idea.

1: _____

_____

2: _____

_____

The Shining Light Day Center

As parents, the wellbeing of your children is very important. It is important to keep them happy and healthy. It is also important to make sure their bodies and minds are active. It is especially important for children under the age of five. During this time, children can learn good fitness habits that they will keep for life.

During this time, children also learn quickly. They are at a special age where they take in information quickly. They also develop skills easier. It is important to find time to develop both their bodies and minds.

As parents, it can be hard to find time for all this. At the Shining Light Day Center, we understand this. We have created a range of activities to help your child.

Our activities cover many different areas. We want to help children think and learn. We want to help children learn to work with others. We want to help children learn to read and speak. We also want to help children be fit and healthy. Our activities include classes, games, and time for free play. These keep the child interested. At the same time, they are learning and growing.

Our programs are aimed at children between the ages of 3 and 5. Children will enjoy playing with others. They will learn basic math and English skills. Our program helps children start grade school. Think of it as a head start for your child!

Our classes are held at two different times. On weekdays, classes are held from noon to 3 p.m. On weekends, classes are held from 9 to 11 a.m. This gives you a lot of choice as a parent. You can choose the day and time that best suits you.

All parents should consider the Shining Light Day Center. It will give your child the best head start in life. Visit our website today to learn more. You can also call a member of our staff to discuss your child's future. You can also drop in any time to watch a class.

Learning Activity	Details
Storytelling	Children listen to stories being told. They answer questions about the story. Then they help write the ending to the story.
Telling Time	Students learn counting skills by using clocks. They count hours and minutes.
Hide and Seek	Children must find blocks hidden in our outdoor play areas. They race to find all the blocks of their color.
Puppet Show	Children use hand puppets to act out stories. They work in pairs.

23 Read this sentence from the passage.

They also develop skills easier.

Which word means the opposite of <u>easier</u>?

- Ⓐ Simpler
- Ⓑ Harder
- Ⓒ Quicker
- Ⓓ Slower

24 Which two words from the passage have about the same meaning?

- Ⓐ *read, speak*
- Ⓑ *fit, healthy*
- Ⓒ *day, time*
- Ⓓ *learning, school*

25 The passage is most like –

- Ⓐ an essay
- Ⓑ an advertisement
- Ⓒ a short story
- Ⓓ a news article

26 How is the third paragraph mainly organized?

   Ⓐ A problem is described and then a solution is given.

   Ⓑ Events are described in the order they occur.

   Ⓒ Facts are given to support an argument.

   Ⓓ A question is asked and then answered.

27 Read this sentence from the passage.

   You can also drop in any time to watch a class.

   What do the words "drop in" mean?

   Ⓐ Phone

   Ⓑ Check

   Ⓒ Visit

   Ⓓ Watch

28 The passage was probably written mainly to –

   Ⓐ encourage parents to send their children to the day center

   Ⓑ compare the day center with grade school

   Ⓒ describe why the day center was started

   Ⓓ inform parents about the benefits of learning

29 The web below describes the different areas covered by the activities. Complete the chart by listing **two** more areas covered by the activities.

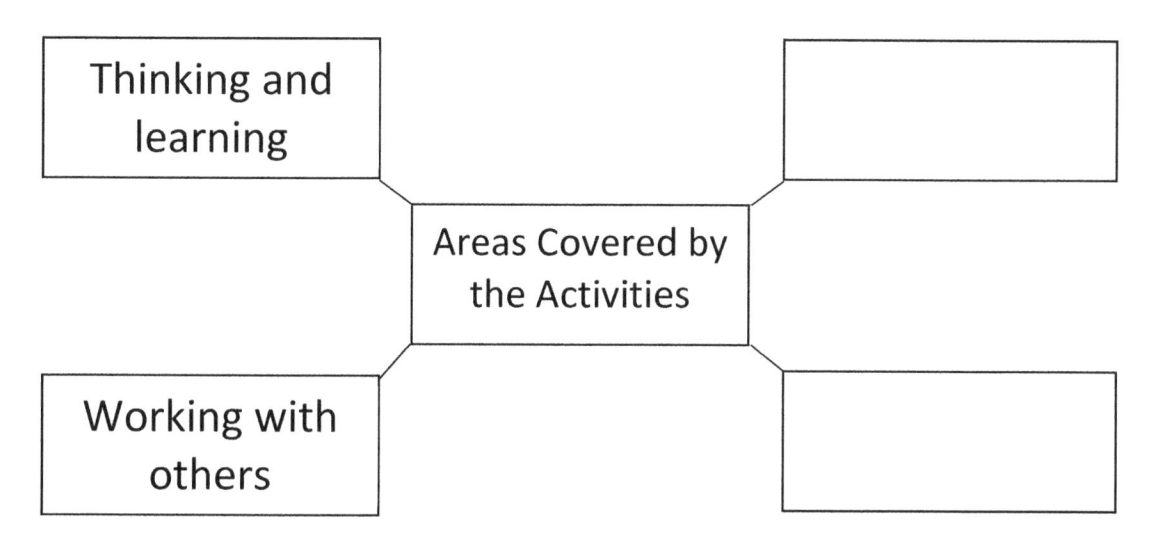

```
┌─────────────┐                              ┌─────────────┐
│ Thinking and│                              │             │
│  learning   │                              │             │
└─────────────┘                              └─────────────┘
              ╲                            ╱
               ┌──────────────────┐
               │ Areas Covered by │
               │  the Activities  │
               └──────────────────┘
              ╱                            ╲
┌─────────────┐                              ┌─────────────┐
│Working with │                              │             │
│   others    │                              │             │
└─────────────┘                              └─────────────┘
```

30 What do you think the author's main purpose for including the table is? Use details from the passage in your answer.

_____

_____

_____

_____

_____

FSA Practice Test Book, English Language Arts, Grade 3

31 Which sentence is included mainly to persuade the reader?

Ⓐ   As parents, it can be hard to find time for all this.

Ⓑ   Our programs are aimed at children between the ages of 3 and 5.

Ⓒ   On weekdays, classes are held from noon to 3 p.m.

Ⓓ   It will give your child the best head start in life.

32 Which activity from the table would be most likely to develop math skills?

Ⓐ   Storytelling

Ⓑ   Telling Time

Ⓒ   Hide and Seek

Ⓓ   Puppet Show

33 Read these sentences from the first paragraph.

> **It is also important to make sure their bodies and minds are active. It is especially important for children under the age of five.**

List **two** reasons the author gives to show why it is important for children under the age of five.

1: _____

2: _____

34 The passage describes many benefits of sending children to the Shining Light Day Center. Describe at least **three** benefits to children of going to the Shining Light Day Center. Use details from the passage in your answer.

The passage below contains errors. The words or phrases that are incorrect are underlined. For each word or phrase underlined, answer the question below.

Volcanoes

Hot magma and gases build up inside the earth's crust. Every now and then, it <u>bersts</u> out from under the surface. The result is a volcano. When a volcano blows, rocks and ash can be <u>throwed</u> out high into the atmosphere. Quite <u>amazing</u>, it can reach many miles high.

A volcano forms when <u>their</u> is magma under the surface. Magma is melted rock <u>beneeth</u> the earth's surface. When the magma is above the earth's surface, it is called lava. If you touched lava with a steel rod, the steel rod would melt in seconds. It's hard to imagine, <u>so</u> that's how hot lava is.

35   What is the correct way to spell <u>bersts</u>? Write your answer below.

_____

36   Which of these should replace <u>throwed</u>?
  Ⓐ   threw
  Ⓑ   throw
  Ⓒ   thrown
  Ⓓ   throwing

37 Which of these should replace amazing?

Ⓐ amaze

Ⓑ amazed

Ⓒ amazingly

Ⓓ amazement

38 As it is used in the sentence, what is the correct spelling of their? Write your answer below.

_____

39 Which of these should replace beneeth?

Ⓐ beneith

Ⓑ benieth

Ⓒ benaeth

Ⓓ beneath

40 Which of these should replace so?

Ⓐ and

Ⓑ but

Ⓒ for

Ⓓ or

END OF SESSION 1

Florida Standards Assessment

English Language Arts

Practice Test 3

Session 2

Instructions

Read each passage and answer the questions that follow it.

For each multiple-choice question, fill in the circle for the correct answer. For other types of questions, follow the instructions given. Some of the questions require a written answer. Write your answer on the lines provided.

The Top of the Tower

Toby had a fear of heights. He had carried it with him since he was an infant. As a teenager, his fear had only become worse. He talked to his father about it one day.

"I have had enough Dad," he said. "I would love to go rock climbing with my friends. But every time I get too high, I feel sick."

His dad paused as he thought about his son's problem.

"Well Toby," he said quietly, "I can help you. But you will need to face your fear. Are you ready?"

Toby was quiet for a moment.

"I am ready!" he replied bravely.

Toby's father picked up the keys and walked toward the front door.

"We're going into the city!" his father said.

Toby knew what was coming. Toby lived in Paris, France. Located in the heart of Paris, was one of the world's tallest landmarks. It was the Eiffel Tower. Toby knew that visitors were allowed to climb to the very top. The view overlooked the entire city. Nothing was said between the pair as they drove into the city.

They had arrived at the Eiffel Tower when Toby looked up at it and gasped. His stomach turned over.

"I'm not sure if I can do this," he said nervously.

Toby's father sensed his son's worries.

"Don't worry," he said. "I will be with you every step of the way. This is the day that you beat your fears."

Toby stared up at the giant tower. He took a deep breath as they stepped through the entrance. As his father held his hand, they made their way, step by step, towards the top of the building. Once they reached the top, Toby stepped out from the shadows and onto the ledge.

"Wow, Dad!" he said excitedly as he looked over Paris. The city looked so beautiful from the tower that his fear began to fade. He kept his hand firmly on the tower's metal railing just in case. It felt strong and steady. He still felt a small knot of fear in his stomach, but he told himself that he was fine. Just like the tower, he felt strong and steady.

"I told you there was nothing to worry about," his father said.

41 What does the phrase "heart of" mean in the sentence below?

Located in the heart of Paris, was one of the world's tallest landmarks.

- Ⓐ Streets of
- Ⓑ Edge of
- Ⓒ Center of
- Ⓓ City of

42 Read this sentence from the passage.

Nothing was said between the pair as they drove into the city.

Why was Toby most likely quiet?

- Ⓐ He was fighting with his father.
- Ⓑ He was feeling scared.
- Ⓒ He was excited.
- Ⓓ He was having a nap.

43 Based on the second paragraph, what is the main reason Toby wants to change?

- Ⓐ He does not like being teased.
- Ⓑ He wants to make his father proud.
- Ⓒ He is scared that things will get worse.
- Ⓓ He is tired of missing out on doing things.

44 Describe **two** details from the passage that show that Toby feels nervous about climbing the Eiffel Tower.

1: _____

_____

2: _____

_____

45 Read this sentence from the passage.

> **As his father held his hand, they made their way, step by step, towards the top of the building.**

What do the words "step by step" suggest?

Ⓐ They moved quite slowly.

Ⓑ They walked a long way.

Ⓒ They raced each other.

Ⓓ They made a lot of noise.

46 Who is telling the story?

Ⓐ Toby

Ⓑ Toby's father

Ⓒ A friend of Toby's

Ⓓ Someone not in the story

47 The main theme of the passage is about –

- Ⓐ taking chances
- Ⓑ overcoming fears
- Ⓒ making friends
- Ⓓ asking for help

48 In the second last paragraph, Toby is described as feeling "strong and steady." The word <u>steady</u> probably means that he feels –

- Ⓐ scared
- Ⓑ sick
- Ⓒ calm
- Ⓓ joyful

49 Complete these sentences. Write **one** of the words below on each line.

shy   calm   afraid   amazed

brave   silly   kind   rude

When Toby looks up at the tower, he feels _____.

When Toby climbs the tower, he is being _____.

50 How do you think Toby feels at the end of the passage? Use details from the passage to explain your answer.

_____

_____

_____

_____

51 What is Toby's main problem in the passage? How does Toby overcome the problem? Use details from the passage in your answer.

_____

_____

_____

_____

Yard Sales

A yard sale is when you sell items in your front yard. People have yard sales to get rid of unwanted items. It can also be a good way to make some extra money. Here are some tips on how to have a good yard sale.

Finding the Items

1. You need a lot of items to sell. Search your home for all your unwanted items. Make sure everyone in the family joins in. Try to get a large range of items.

2. Clean out the garage or basement. Many people have a store of old stuff somewhere. Offer to clean up this area. As you do, collect everything you think you can sell.

3. Ask other people you know to join in. Many people have junk lying around they want to get rid of. They may be happy to give it to you to sell.

Setting It Up

1. Collect everything you have to sell. It is a good idea to make everything look neat and tidy. If you have clothes, wash them and hang them up. They may not be new clothes, but they'll have to look fresh and clean if you want people to buy them. Clean and dust all the items so they look their best.

2. Set up tables in your front yard to place all the items on. If you are placing items on the ground, put them on a sheet or blanket.

3. People will need to know how much each item is. Put a sticker on each item and write the price on it.

4. Collect some change. People will often pay in notes. Make sure you have plenty of coins to give as change.

Getting a Crowd

1. You want lots of people to come to your yard sale. Here are some things you should do:

- Tell all your friends
- Put notices on notice boards
- Put up flyers
- Put an ad in the local newspaper
- Put a sign at the end of your street

2. Make it easy for people to find the yard sale. Put balloons at the end of your street and in your front yard.

Time to Sell

1. Now it is time to sell your items. Remember that you are selling things you don't really want. Don't try to sell your items for too much. Be open to haggling too. Many people will want a bargain and may not want to pay what you think it's worth. If people suggest a lower price, take it! If people are thinking about buying something, make them a deal.

2. If items are not selling, lower the prices. It is better to sell items for something than to have to pack them all up again.

Popular Yard Sale Items
children's toys
clothes
building materials
furniture
kitchen items
books and movies

52   Read this sentence from the passage.

People often have yard sales to get rid of unwanted items.

What does the word <u>unwanted</u> mean?

Ⓐ   Less wanted

Ⓑ   Used to be wanted

Ⓒ   More wanted

Ⓓ   Not wanted

53   Why should you put balloons in your front yard?

Ⓐ   So people feel good about buying

Ⓑ   So you can sell them

Ⓒ   So people can find your yard sale

Ⓓ   So you can put prices on them

54   If the passage was given another title, which of these would best fit?

Ⓐ   How to Make Money

Ⓑ   How to Hold a Yard Sale

Ⓒ   The Amazing Yard Sale

Ⓓ   Cleaning Up Your House

55 Read this sentence from the passage.

It is a good idea to make everything look neat and tidy.

Which word means the opposite of <u>neat</u>?

- Ⓐ   Messy
- Ⓑ   Clean
- Ⓒ   Dirty
- Ⓓ   Nice

56 Which section of the passage describes how to let people know about your yard sale?

- Ⓐ   Finding the Items
- Ⓑ   Setting It Up
- Ⓒ   Getting a Crowd
- Ⓓ   Time to Sell

57 According to the passage, which of the following should you do first?

- Ⓐ   Set up tables
- Ⓑ   Clean all the items
- Ⓒ   Put stickers on the items
- Ⓓ   Lower the prices

58 How does the information in the table help the reader?

   Ⓐ   It explains how much money can be made.

   Ⓑ   It shows what sort of items to collect.

   Ⓒ   It shows how to price items.

   Ⓓ   It explains why you should have a yard sale.

59 Which phrase from "Time to Sell" best helps you understand the meaning of haggling? Tick the box of the phrase you have selected.

   ☐ "now it is time"

   ☐ "things you don't really want"

   ☐ "many people"

   ☐ "suggest a lower price"

   ☐ "thinking about buying"

60 Describe **two** things the art in the passage helps you understand.

   1: _____

   _____

   2: _____

   _____

61 Draw lines to match each sentence in the first paragraph with its main purpose.

A yard sale is when you sell items in your front yard.	to give a second reason for having a yard sale
People have yard sales to get rid of unwanted items.	to tell what a yard sale is
It can also be a good way to make some extra money.	to give the main reason for having a yard sale
Here are some tips on how to have a good yard sale.	to tell what the passage is about

62 In "Finding the Items," the author suggests that you ask other people to join in. Explain why you think this would be a good idea. Use information from the passage to support your response.

_____

_____

_____

_____

_____

_____

63 Sort the list of things to do below into things that would be best to do in the week before your yard sale and things that would be best to do on the day of your yard sale. Write **three** of the items in each column.

    put up flyers   put balloons up   set up the tables

    tell your friends   put a sign in your street   run a newspaper ad

The Week Before Your Yard Sale	On the Day of Your Yard Sale

The passage below contains errors. The words or phrases that are incorrect are underlined. For each word or phrase underlined, answer the question below.

Stewart the Dragon

Stewart was a <u>very big, green, dragon</u>. He lived in a cave on the top of a hill. The people in the town below were very scared of him. If they ever <u>sore</u> Stewart, they ran inside to hide. This made Stewart very sad. He did not want to hert anybody. He just wanted to be part of the town. It always looked like everyone was having lots of fun.

One night it <u>were</u> very cold, and the people of the town could not start the fire. Stewart went down to the town. He used his fire breath to start the fire. The people of the town realized that Stewart was a helpful and <u>careing</u> dragon. They invited Stewart to come down to the town every night. Stewart started the fire each night. Then he ate and <u>drinked</u> with the villagers, before returning <u>happly</u> to his home.

64 Which of these should replace <u>very big, green, dragon</u>?
- Ⓐ very big green dragon
- Ⓑ very big, green dragon
- Ⓒ very big green, dragon
- Ⓓ very, big green dragon

65 As it is used in the sentence, what is the correct spelling of <u>sore</u>? Write your answer below.

_____

66 Which of these should replace were?

- Ⓐ are
- Ⓑ be
- Ⓒ is
- Ⓓ was

67 Which of these should replace careing?

- Ⓐ caring
- Ⓑ carring
- Ⓒ cearing
- Ⓓ cearring

68 Which of these should replace drinked?

- Ⓐ drank
- Ⓑ drink
- Ⓒ drinking
- Ⓓ dranked

69 Which of these should replace happly?

- Ⓐ hapilly
- Ⓑ happilly
- Ⓒ happily
- Ⓓ hapily

FSA Practice Test Book, English Language Arts, Grade 3

The questions below are answered after listening to a passage. Ask someone to read you the passage "The Dog and the River" from the back of this book. Then answer the questions below.

Questions for "The Dog and the River"

70 What is the main lesson the dog learns in the passage?

Ⓐ Bigger is usually better.

Ⓑ Be thankful for what you have.

Ⓒ Be careful when crossing rivers.

Ⓓ Fighting does not achieve anything.

71 Which of the following is the best summary of the passage?

Ⓐ A dog with a small piece of meat thinks his reflection is a dog with a large piece of meat. He tries to get the large piece and ends up with no meat.

Ⓑ A dog sees another dog with a better piece of meat. He drops his own piece. He loses the fight with the other dog.

Ⓒ A dog thinks he sees a dog with a larger piece of meat. He drops his own meat. Then he realizes that the other piece of meat is not real. He regrets the decision that he made.

Ⓓ A dog is crossing a river with a small piece of meat. He drops the meat into the river. He is unable to get it back.

72 The main flaw of the dog is that he is –

Ⓐ clumsy

Ⓑ jealous

Ⓒ rude

Ⓓ foolish

The questions below are answered after listening to a passage. Ask someone to read you the passage "Hillary Clinton" from the back of this book. Then answer the questions below.

Questions for "Hillary Clinton"

73 Where would this passage most likely be found?

- Ⓐ In an encyclopedia
- Ⓑ In a travel guide
- Ⓒ In a newspaper
- Ⓓ In a book of short stories

74 Place Hillary Clinton's roles in politics in order from first to last. Write the numbers 1, 2, 3, and 4 on the lines to show your choices.

____ Senator for New York

____ First Lady

____ Secretary of State

____ Candidate for president

75 Which of these would make the best opening sentence for a summary of the passage?

- Ⓐ Hillary Clinton has had a successful and varied career in politics.
- Ⓑ Hillary Clinton met Bill Clinton while studying at Yale Law School.
- Ⓒ While First Lady, Hillary Clinton played an active political role.
- Ⓓ In 2008, some considered that Hillary Clinton could become America's first female president.

END OF SESSION 2

ANSWER KEY

Language Arts Florida Standards (LAFS)

In 2014, the state of Florida adopted the Language Arts Florida Standards (LAFS). These standards describe what students are expected to know. Student learning throughout the year is based on these standards, and all the questions on the Florida Standards Assessments (FSA) cover these standards. All the exercises and questions in this book cover the Language Arts Florida Standards.

Just like on the real test, the majority of the questions cover reading standards. However, language and speaking and listening standards are also covered. The editing tasks on each practice test cover language standards, and the listening tasks cover speaking and listening standards. The answer key that follows lists the main standard assessed by each question.

Scoring Open Response Questions

This practice test book includes open response questions, where students provide a written answer to a question. The answer key gives guidance on how to score these questions. Use the criteria listed as a guide to scoring these questions, and as a guide for giving the student advice on how to improve an answer.

Practice Test 1, Session 1

Question	Answer	Language Arts Florida Standard
1	A	Determine the meaning of words and phrases as they are used in a text, distinguishing literal from nonliteral language.
2	C	Determine the meaning of words and phrases as they are used in a text, distinguishing literal from nonliteral language.
3	See Below	Ask and answer questions to demonstrate understanding of a text, referring explicitly to the text as the basis for the answers.
4	D	Recount stories; determine the central message, lesson, or moral and explain how it is conveyed through key details in the text.
5	A	Recount stories, including fables, folktales, and myths from diverse cultures; determine the central message, lesson, or moral and explain how it is conveyed through key details in the text.
6	C	Determine the meaning of words and phrases as they are used in a text, distinguishing literal from nonliteral language.
7	D	Read and comprehend literature, including stories, dramas, and poetry independently and proficiently.
8	B	Describe characters in a story (e.g., their traits, motivations, or feelings) and explain how their actions contribute to the sequence of events.
9	A	Describe characters in a story (e.g., their traits, motivations, or feelings) and explain how their actions contribute to the sequence of events.
10	C	Recount stories; determine the central message, lesson, or moral and explain how it is conveyed through key details in the text.
11	See Below	Recount stories; determine the central message, lesson, or moral and explain how it is conveyed through key details in the text.
12	See Below	Distinguish their own point of view from that of the narrator or those of the characters.
13	C	Determine the meaning of general academic and domain-specific words and phrases in a text.
14	A	Use text features and search tools (e.g., key words, sidebars, hyperlinks) to locate information relevant to a given topic efficiently.
15	A	Determine the main idea of a text; recount the key details and explain how they support the main idea.
16	Step 1	Describe the relationship between a series of historical events, scientific ideas or concepts, or steps in technical procedures in a text, using language that pertains to time, sequence, and cause/effect.
17	B	Determine the meaning of general academic and domain-specific words and phrases in a text.
18	See Below	Describe the relationship between a series of historical events, scientific ideas or concepts, or steps in technical procedures in a text, using language that pertains to time, sequence, and cause/effect.
19	C	Ask and answer questions to demonstrate understanding of a text, referring explicitly to the text as the basis for the answers.
20	B	Describe the logical connection between particular sentences and paragraphs in a text (e.g., comparison, cause/effect, first/second/third in a sequence).
21	See Below	Determine the main idea of a text; recount the key details and explain how they support the main idea.
22	See Below	Describe the relationship between a series of historical events, scientific ideas or concepts, or steps in technical procedures in a text, using language that pertains to time, sequence, and cause/effect.
23	See Below	Distinguish their own point of view from that of the author of a text.

24	B	Describe characters in a story (e.g., their traits, motivations, or feelings) and explain how their actions contribute to the sequence of events.
25	C	Ask and answer questions to demonstrate understanding of a text, referring explicitly to the text as the basis for the answers.
26	B	Refer to parts of stories, dramas, and poems when writing or speaking about a text, using terms such as chapter, scene, and stanza; describe how each successive part builds on earlier sections.
27	A	Distinguish their own point of view from that of the narrator or those of the characters.
28	B	Ask and answer questions to demonstrate understanding of a text, referring explicitly to the text as the basis for the answers.
29	See Below	Recount stories, including fables, folktales, and myths from diverse cultures; determine the central message, lesson, or moral and explain how it is conveyed through key details in the text.
30	D	Ask and answer questions to demonstrate understanding of a text, referring explicitly to the text as the basis for the answers.
31	B	Determine the meaning of words and phrases as they are used in a text, distinguishing literal from nonliteral language.
32	B	Ask and answer questions to demonstrate understanding of a text, referring explicitly to the text as the basis for the answers.
33	C	Explain how specific aspects of a text's illustrations contribute to what is conveyed by the words in a story.
34	See Below	Describe characters in a story (e.g., their traits, motivations, or feelings) and explain how their actions contribute to the sequence of events.
35	B	Demonstrate command of the conventions of standard English grammar and usage when writing or speaking.
36	C	Demonstrate command of the conventions of standard English capitalization, punctuation, and spelling when writing.
37	D	Demonstrate command of the conventions of standard English grammar and usage when writing or speaking.
38	A	Demonstrate command of the conventions of standard English grammar and usage when writing or speaking.
39	tomorrow	Demonstrate command of the conventions of standard English capitalization, punctuation, and spelling when writing.
40	A	Demonstrate command of the conventions of standard English grammar and usage when writing or speaking.

Q3.
Give a score of 0, 1, 2, or 3 based on how many correct examples are listed. Possible answers are listed below.
- Singing, running fast, playing volleyball, reading fast, choosing clothes

Q11.
Give a score of 0, 1, or 2 based on how well the answer meets the criteria listed below.
- It should give a reasonable explanation of why the student chose the title.
- It should relate the title to the theme of the passage.
- It should use relevant details from the passage.

Q12.
Give a score of 0, 1, or 2 based on how well the answer meets the criteria listed below.
- It should give a reasonable description of how the girls competing could be good for them.
- The answer may refer to how it makes the girls try harder or how it encourages them to do better.

Q18.
Give a score of 0, 1, 2, or 3 based on how many sentences are written in the correct place in the diagram.
- It is too sour. → Add sugar. / It is too sweet. → Add lemon juice. / It is too strong. → Add water.

Q21.
Give a score of 0, 1, or 2 based on how many relevant examples are given.
- Any reasonable answer can be accepted as long as it is based on information in the passage.
- The student may refer to setting up a lemonade at the friend's house, having help to make the lemonade, having someone to help decorate the stand, or selling other products the friend makes.

Q22.
The student should complete the chart in the order below. Give a score of 0.5 for each item correctly ordered.
- sugar → boiling water → lemon juice → cold water

Q23.
Give a score of 0, 1, or 2 based on how well the answer meets the criteria listed below.
- It should state whether or not the student feels it would be worth it to make lemonade.
- It should provide a fully-supported explanation of why or why not.

Q29.
Give a score of 0, 1, or 2 based on how many relevant details are given.
- Possible details could refer to how she paces up and down, how she keeps asking where he is, how she searches the crowd, or how she stands tall to try to see every person coming through the gate.

Q34.
Give a score of 0, 1, or 2 based on how well the answer meets the criteria listed below.
- It should provide a reasonable analysis of what the father's actions show about how he feels.
- It may refer to how he drops his bags or to how he sweeps his daughters into his arms.
- It should describe how he feels excited, overjoyed, or relieved.

Practice Test 1, Session 2

Question	Answer	Language Arts Florida Standard
41	C	Determine the meaning of general academic and domain-specific words and phrases in a text.
42	B	Determine the meaning of general academic and domain-specific words and phrases in a text.
43	C	Ask and answer questions to demonstrate understanding of a text, referring explicitly to the text as the basis for the answers.
44	A	Determine the main idea of a text; recount the key details and explain how they support the main idea.
45	D	Determine the main idea of a text; recount the key details and explain how they support the main idea.
46	A	Describe the logical connection between particular sentences and paragraphs in a text (e.g., comparison, cause/effect, first/second/third in a sequence).
47	Standing up for yourself	Use text features and search tools (e.g., key words, sidebars, hyperlinks) to locate information relevant to a given topic efficiently.
48	C	Distinguish their own point of view from that of the author of a text.
49	See Below	Determine the main idea of a text; recount the key details and explain how they support the main idea.
50	C	Determine the meaning of words and phrases as they are used in a text, distinguishing literal from nonliteral language.
51	famous well-known	Determine the meaning of words and phrases as they are used in a text, distinguishing literal from nonliteral language.
52	A	Describe characters in a story (e.g., their traits, motivations, or feelings) and explain how their actions contribute to the sequence of events.
53	B	Ask and answer questions to demonstrate understanding of a text, referring explicitly to the text as the basis for the answers.
54	From top to bottom: 3, 2, 4, 1	Refer to parts of stories, dramas, and poems when writing or speaking about a text, using terms such as chapter, scene, and stanza; describe how each successive part builds on earlier sections.
55	B	Recount stories, including fables, folktales, and myths from diverse cultures; determine the central message, lesson, or moral and explain how it is conveyed through key details in the text.
56	C	Refer to parts of stories, dramas, and poems when writing or speaking about a text, using terms such as chapter, scene, and stanza; describe how each successive part builds on earlier sections.
57	D	Describe characters in a story (e.g., their traits, motivations, or feelings) and explain how their actions contribute to the sequence of events.
58	Sentences 3 and 4	Ask and answer questions to demonstrate understanding of a text, referring explicitly to the text as the basis for the answers.
59	See Below	Recount stories, including fables, folktales, and myths from diverse cultures; determine the central message, lesson, or moral and explain how it is conveyed through key details in the text.
60	See Below	Describe characters in a story (e.g., their traits, motivations, or feelings) and explain how their actions contribute to the sequence of events.
61	B	Demonstrate command of the conventions of standard English capitalization, punctuation, and spelling when writing.
62	B	Demonstrate command of the conventions of standard English grammar and usage when writing or speaking.
63	A	Demonstrate command of the conventions of standard English capitalization, punctuation, and spelling when writing.

64	South America	Demonstrate command of the conventions of standard English capitalization, punctuation, and spelling when writing.
65	interesting	Demonstrate command of the conventions of standard English capitalization, punctuation, and spelling when writing.
66	D	Demonstrate command of the conventions of standard English capitalization, punctuation, and spelling when writing.
67	B	Ask and answer questions about information from a speaker, offering appropriate elaboration and detail.
68	D	Determine the main ideas and supporting details of a text read aloud or information presented in diverse media and formats, including visually, quantitatively, and orally.
69	B	Ask and answer questions about information from a speaker, offering appropriate elaboration and detail.
70	A	Ask and answer questions about information from a speaker, offering appropriate elaboration and detail.
71	A	Determine the main ideas and supporting details of a text read aloud or information presented in diverse media and formats, including visually, quantitatively, and orally.
72	A	Ask and answer questions about information from a speaker, offering appropriate elaboration and detail.

Q49.
Give a score of 0, 1, or 2 based on how well the answer meets the criteria listed below.
- It should describe the benefits of increasing the length of the lunch break.
- The benefits described should be based on the argument from the passage.
- It should use relevant details from the passage.

Q59.
Give a score of 0, 1, or 2 based on how well the answer meets the criteria listed below.
- It should describe the lesson that Kevin learns in the story. The lesson should be not to be mean to others, to focus on being known for something positive, or how being funny can become nasty.
- It should use relevant details from the passage.

Q60.
Give a score of 0, 1, or 2 based on how well the answer meets the criteria listed below.
- It should make a prediction about whether or not Kevin will keep playing jokes.
- It should provide a fully-supported explanation to support the prediction.
- It should use relevant details from the passage.

Practice Test 2, Session 1

Question	Answer	Language Arts Florida Standard
1	C	Determine the meaning of general academic and domain-specific words and phrases in a text.
2	A	Determine the meaning of general academic and domain-specific words and phrases in a text.
3	B	Ask and answer questions to demonstrate understanding of a text, referring explicitly to the text as the basis for the answers.
4	A	Describe the logical connection between particular sentences and paragraphs in a text (e.g., comparison, cause/effect, first/second/third in a sequence).
5	B	Determine the main idea of a text; recount the key details and explain how they support the main idea.
6	See Below	Determine the main idea of a text; recount the key details and explain how they support the main idea.
7	See Below	Ask and answer questions to demonstrate understanding of a text, referring explicitly to the text as the basis for the answers.
8	B	Describe the relationship between a series of historical events, scientific ideas or concepts, or steps in technical procedures in a text, using language that pertains to time, sequence, and cause/effect.
9	B	Distinguish their own point of view from that of the author of a text.
10	D	Determine the meaning of general academic and domain-specific words and phrases in a text.
11	See Below	Describe the relationship between a series of historical events, scientific ideas or concepts, or steps in technical procedures in a text, using language that pertains to time, sequence, and cause/effect.
12	See Below	Use information gained from illustrations and the words in a text to demonstrate understanding of the text.
13	B	Determine the meaning of words and phrases as they are used in a text, distinguishing literal from nonliteral language.
14	decision choice	Determine the meaning of words and phrases as they are used in a text, distinguishing literal from nonliteral language.
15	third pair	Ask and answer questions to demonstrate understanding of a text, referring explicitly to the text as the basis for the answers.
16	A	Recount stories, including fables, folktales, and myths from diverse cultures; determine the central message, lesson, or moral and explain how it is conveyed through key details in the text.
17	A	Determine the meaning of words and phrases as they are used in a text, distinguishing literal from nonliteral language.
18	A	Describe characters in a story (e.g., their traits, motivations, or feelings) and explain how their actions contribute to the sequence of events.
19	A	Refer to parts of stories, dramas, and poems when writing or speaking about a text, using terms such as chapter, scene, and stanza; describe how each successive part builds on earlier sections.
20	See Below	Recount stories, including fables, folktales, and myths from diverse cultures; determine the central message, lesson, or moral and explain how it is conveyed through key details in the text.
21	D	Distinguish their own point of view from that of the narrator or those of the characters.
22	See Below	Describe characters in a story (e.g., their traits, motivations, or feelings) and explain how their actions contribute to the sequence of events.
23	See Below	Refer to parts of stories, dramas, and poems when writing or speaking about a text, using terms such as chapter, scene, and stanza; describe how each successive part builds on earlier sections.

24	B	Determine the meaning of general academic and domain-specific words and phrases in a text.
25	B	Use text features and search tools (e.g., key words, sidebars, hyperlinks) to locate information relevant to a given topic efficiently.
26	A	Describe the relationship between a series of historical events, scientific ideas or concepts, or steps in technical procedures in a text, using language that pertains to time, sequence, and cause/effect.
27	A	Determine the main idea of a text; recount the key details and explain how they support the main idea.
28	B	Determine the meaning of general academic and domain-specific words and phrases in a text.
29	Step 3	Describe the relationship between a series of historical events, scientific ideas or concepts, or steps in technical procedures in a text, using language that pertains to time, sequence, and cause/effect.
30	C	Use information gained from illustrations and the words in a text to demonstrate understanding of the text.
31	B	Use information gained from illustrations and the words in a text to demonstrate understanding of the text.
32	A	Ask and answer questions to demonstrate understanding of a text, referring explicitly to the text as the basis for the answers.
33	See Below	Use information gained from illustrations and the words in a text to demonstrate understanding of the text.
34	See Below	Describe the logical connection between particular sentences and paragraphs in a text (e.g., comparison, cause/effect, first/second/third in a sequence).
35	See Below	Use text features and search tools (e.g., key words, sidebars, hyperlinks) to locate information relevant to a given topic efficiently.
36	D	Demonstrate command of the conventions of standard English grammar and usage when writing or speaking.
37	C	Demonstrate command of the conventions of standard English capitalization, punctuation, and spelling when writing.
38	A	Demonstrate command of the conventions of standard English grammar and usage when writing or speaking.
39	A	Demonstrate command of the conventions of standard English capitalization, punctuation, and spelling when writing.
40	"I guess it's not that simple," said the donkey.	Demonstrate command of the conventions of standard English capitalization, punctuation, and spelling when writing.

Q6.
Give a score of 0, 1, or 2 based on how many relevant supporting details are given.
- The supporting details listed could be that Rafael Nadal beat Roger Federer at Wimbledon in 2008 and 2010, that Nadal beat Roger in 6 out of 8 Grand Slam finals, that Nadal became world number one, or that Roger will have to beat Nadal to become number one again.

Q7.
Give a score of 0.5 for each fact circled. Give a score of 0, 1, or 2 based on how many additional facts are listed.
- The second and third sentences should be circled.
- Any factual detail from the passage can be accepted.

Q11.
Give a score of 0, 1, or 2 based on how well the answer meets the criteria listed below.
- It should provide a reasonable explanation of why the 2008 Wimbledon final was important.
- It should include two reasons that the final was important. Possible reasons could refer to how Nadal stopped Roger from winning six times, how it was a tough match, how it started a row between them, or how some people think it was the best match ever played.

Q12.
Give a score of 0, 1, 2, or 3 based on how well the answer meets the criteria listed below.
- It should use relevant details to explain how the author shows that Federer is a successful tennis player.
- The details may include that he has been the world number one, that he was world number one for 237 weeks, that he has won 16 Grand Slam finals, or that he has won Wimbledon six times.

Q20.
Give a score of 0, 1, or 2 based on how well the answer meets the criteria listed below.
- It should provide a reasonable explanation of why the last paragraph is important to the main idea.
- The answer should refer to how the last paragraph shows that Steven's bold decision paid off.

Q22.
Give a score of 0, 1, or 2 based on how well the answer meets the criteria listed below.
- It should make a reasonable prediction about whether Steven team's would have won without him.
- Any prediction can be accepted as long as it is explained and supported with details from the passage.

Q23.
Give a score of 0, 1, or 2 based on how well the answer meets the criteria listed below.
- It should provide an analysis of what the paragraph reveals about Steven.
- The answer may refer to how it shows that he knew playing was a risk to himself, how he thought carefully about his decision, or how he put the needs of his team first.

Q33.
Give a score of 0, 1, or 2 based on how many acceptable features are listed.
- Any feature that helps show that the passage is a recipe can be accepted.
- The features could be broad, such as that the passage tells how to make a food or gives directions.
- The features could be specific, such as that the passage has a section titled "What to Do," has steps to follow, or includes a picture of making food.

Q34.
Give a score of 0, 1, or 2 based on how many correct reasons are given.
- Possible answers include that children like them, that they are crunchy, that the flavor is a hit, or that they are easy to make.

Q35.
Give a score of 0, 1, 2, or 3 based on how well the answer meets the criteria listed below.
- It should identify three tasks that would have to be done carefully and give a reasonable explanation of why you have to be careful and what you have to do to stop things going wrong.
- The three tasks could be based on softening the butter in step 2, cleaning your hands before mixing in step 2, not getting water in the chocolate in step 4, letting the chocolate cool in step 5, or making sure the rice crispy cake is covered in chocolate in step 5.
- It should use relevant details from the passage.

Practice Test 2, Session 2

Question	Answer	Language Arts Florida Standard
41	C	Ask and answer questions to demonstrate understanding of a text, referring explicitly to the text as the basis for the answers.
42	A	Determine the meaning of words and phrases as they are used in a text, distinguishing literal from nonliteral language.
43	C	Refer to parts of stories, dramas, and poems when writing or speaking about a text, using terms such as chapter, scene, and stanza; describe how each successive part builds on earlier sections.
44	C	Determine the meaning of words and phrases as they are used in a text, distinguishing literal from nonliteral language.
45	D	Determine the meaning of words and phrases as they are used in a text, distinguishing literal from nonliteral language.
46	D	Recount stories, including fables, folktales, and myths from diverse cultures; determine the central message, lesson, or moral and explain how it is conveyed through key details in the text.
47	See Below	Explain how specific aspects of a text's illustrations contribute to what is conveyed by the words in a story.
48	See Below	Ask and answer questions to demonstrate understanding of a text, referring explicitly to the text as the basis for the answers.
49	See Below	Distinguish their own point of view from that of the narrator or those of the characters.
50	A	Determine the meaning of general academic and domain-specific words and phrases in a text.
51	A	Determine the meaning of general academic and domain-specific words and phrases in a text.
52	D	Describe the relationship between a series of historical events, scientific ideas or concepts, or steps in technical procedures in a text, using language that pertains to time, sequence, and cause/effect.
53	See Below	Describe the logical connection between particular sentences and paragraphs in a text (e.g., comparison, cause/effect, first/second/third in a sequence).
54	See Below	Use text features and search tools (e.g., key words, sidebars, hyperlinks) to locate information relevant to a given topic efficiently.
55	C	Use information gained from illustrations and the words in a text to demonstrate understanding of the text.
56	A	Determine the main idea of a text; recount the key details and explain how they support the main idea.
57	C	Use text features and search tools (e.g., key words, sidebars, hyperlinks) to locate information relevant to a given topic efficiently.
58	See Below	Ask and answer questions to demonstrate understanding of a text, referring explicitly to the text as the basis for the answers.
59	See Below	Distinguish their own point of view from that of the author of a text.
60	A Day of Learning	Demonstrate command of the conventions of standard English capitalization, punctuation, and spelling when writing.
61	C	Demonstrate command of the conventions of standard English grammar and usage when writing or speaking.
62	B	Demonstrate command of the conventions of standard English grammar and usage when writing or speaking.
63	A	Demonstrate command of the conventions of standard English capitalization, punctuation, and spelling when writing.
64	B	Demonstrate command of the conventions of standard English grammar and usage when writing or speaking.

65	more	Demonstrate command of the conventions of standard English capitalization, punctuation, and spelling when writing.
66	D	Determine the main ideas and supporting details of a text read aloud or information presented in diverse media and formats, including visually, quantitatively, and orally.
67	A	Ask and answer questions about information from a speaker, offering appropriate elaboration and detail.
68	D	Determine the main ideas and supporting details of a text read aloud or information presented in diverse media and formats, including visually, quantitatively, and orally.
69	D	Ask and answer questions about information from a speaker, offering appropriate elaboration and detail.
70	A	Determine the main ideas and supporting details of a text read aloud or information presented in diverse media and formats, including visually, quantitatively, and orally.

Q47.
Give a score of 0, 1, or 2 based on how well the answer meets the criteria listed below.
- It should provide a reasonable description of what the photograph helps readers understand.
- The answer could refer to how the photograph shows how bees make honey or to how it shows how beekeepers protect themselves.

Q48.
Give a score of 0, 1, 2, or 3 based on how many correct facts are listed in the diagram.
- Any detail included in the poem or caption can be accepted as long as it is factual and not an opinion.

Q49.
Give a score of 0, 1, or 2 based on how well the answer meets the criteria listed below.
- It should provide a reasonable analysis of how the point of view affects the poem.
- The answer should include an explanation of how the point of view influences whether or not readers can take the poem seriously.
- It should use relevant details from the poem.

Q53.
Give a score of 0.5 for each relevant sentence circled. Give a score of 0, 1, or 2 for the explanation.
- Any of the last 4 sentences can be accepted.
- The student should provide a reasonable explanation of why the two sentences were chosen and how they show the reason for writing the letter.

Q54.
Give a score of 1 for each book added to the table correctly. The correct books are listed below.
- Favorite Book: *The Shining Light*
- First Book Read: *The Singing Swordfish*

Q58.
Give a score of 0, 1, or 2 based on how many relevant reasons are given.
- Possible reasons include that it was well-written, that the pictures were good, or that it made him laugh.

Q59.
Give a score of 0, 1, or 2 based on how well the answer meets the criteria listed below.
- It should give an opinion on whether or not Simeon would feel good after reading the letter.
- It should provide a fully-supported explanation to support the opinion.

FSA Practice Test Book, English Language Arts, Grade 3

Practice Test 3, Session 1

Question	Answer	Language Arts Florida Standard
1	C	Determine the meaning of general academic and domain-specific words and phrases in a text.
2	C	Determine the meaning of general academic and domain-specific words and phrases in a text.
3	A	Use text features and search tools (e.g., key words, sidebars, hyperlinks) to locate information relevant to a given topic efficiently.
4	B	Describe the relationship between a series of historical events, scientific ideas or concepts, or steps in technical procedures in a text, using language that pertains to time, sequence, and cause/effect.
5	B	Ask and answer questions to demonstrate understanding of a text, referring explicitly to the text as the basis for the answers.
6	D	Determine the main idea of a text; recount the key details and explain how they support the main idea.
7	See Below	Use text features and search tools (e.g., key words, sidebars, hyperlinks) to locate information relevant to a given topic efficiently.
8	A	Determine the meaning of general academic and domain-specific words and phrases in a text.
9	See Below	Describe the logical connection between particular sentences and paragraphs in a text (e.g., comparison, cause/effect, first/second/third in a sequence).
10	See Below	Use information gained from illustrations and the words in a text to demonstrate understanding of the text.
11	See Below	Distinguish their own point of view from that of the author of a text.
12	B	Determine the meaning of words and phrases as they are used in a text, distinguishing literal from nonliteral language.
13	C	Ask and answer questions to demonstrate understanding of a text, referring explicitly to the text as the basis for the answers.
14	2	Refer to parts of stories, dramas, and poems when writing or speaking about a text, using terms such as chapter, scene, and stanza; describe how each successive part builds on earlier sections.
15	A	Determine the meaning of words and phrases as they are used in a text, distinguishing literal from nonliteral language.
16	C	Refer to parts of stories, dramas, and poems when writing or speaking about a text, using terms such as chapter, scene, and stanza; describe how each successive part builds on earlier sections.
17	C	Recount stories, including fables, folktales, and myths from diverse cultures; determine the central message, lesson, or moral and explain how it is conveyed through key details in the text.
18	A	Recount stories, including fables, folktales, and myths from diverse cultures; determine the central message, lesson, or moral and explain how it is conveyed through key details in the text.
19	little mighty	Refer to parts of stories, dramas, and poems when writing or speaking about a text, using terms such as chapter, scene, and stanza; describe how each successive part builds on earlier sections.
20	See Below	Recount stories, including fables, folktales, and myths from diverse cultures; determine the central message, lesson, or moral and explain how it is conveyed through key details in the text.
21	See Below	Explain how specific aspects of a text's illustrations contribute to what is conveyed by the words in a story.
22	See Below	Ask and answer questions to demonstrate understanding of a text, referring explicitly to the text as the basis for the answers.
23	B	Determine the meaning of general academic and domain-specific words and phrases in a text.

FSA Practice Test Book, English Language Arts, Grade 3

24	B	Determine the meaning of general academic and domain-specific words and phrases in a text.
25	B	Ask and answer questions to demonstrate understanding of a text, referring explicitly to the text as the basis for the answers.
26	A	Describe the logical connection between particular sentences and paragraphs in a text (e.g., comparison, cause/effect, first/second/third in a sequence).
27	C	Determine the meaning of general academic and domain-specific words and phrases in a text.
28	A	Determine the main idea of a text; recount the key details and explain how they support the main idea.
29	See Below	Use text features and search tools (e.g., key words, sidebars, hyperlinks) to locate information relevant to a given topic efficiently.
30	See Below	Use information gained from illustrations and the words in a text to demonstrate understanding of the text.
31	D	Describe the logical connection between particular sentences and paragraphs in a text (e.g., comparison, cause/effect, first/second/third in a sequence).
32	B	Ask and answer questions to demonstrate understanding of a text, referring explicitly to the text as the basis for the answers.
33	See Below	Determine the main idea of a text; recount the key details and explain how they support the main idea.
34	See Below	Use information gained from illustrations and the words in a text to demonstrate understanding of the text.
35	bursts	Demonstrate command of the conventions of standard English capitalization, punctuation, and spelling when writing.
36	C	Demonstrate command of the conventions of standard English grammar and usage when writing or speaking.
37	C	Demonstrate command of the conventions of standard English grammar and usage when writing or speaking.
38	there	Demonstrate command of the conventions of standard English capitalization, punctuation, and spelling when writing.
39	D	Demonstrate command of the conventions of standard English capitalization, punctuation, and spelling when writing.
40	B	Demonstrate command of the conventions of standard English grammar and usage when writing or speaking.

Q7.
Give a score of 0.5 for each section correctly listed. The possible sections are listed below.
- news, sport, home, travel, food, art, fashion, movies, or puzzles

Q9.
Give a score of 0, 1, or 2 based on how well the answer meets the criteria listed below.
- It should provide a reasonable explanation of the importance of the second sentence.
- The answer should show an understanding that the detail explains what a Pulitzer Prize is, shows the meaning of winning a Pulitzer Prize, or shows that *The New York Times* is known for excellent reporting.

Q10.
Give a score of 0, 1, or 2 based on how many correct differences are given.
- Possible answers include that it now costs more, that it sells fewer copies than it once did, or that it has to compete with online sites that offer news for free.

Q11.
Give a score of 0, 1, or 2 based on how well the answer meets the criteria listed below.
- It should state which details the student found most interesting.
- It should provide a fully-supported explanation of why the student found those details interesting.

Q20.
Give a score of 0, 1, or 2 based on how well the answer meets the criteria listed below.
- It should explain that water, sand, and minutes all make up something much larger than themselves.

Q21.
Give a score of 0, 1, or 2 based on how well the answer meets the criteria listed below.
- It should identify the main idea as being about how little things can lead to greater things over time.
- It should show an understanding that the canyon is an example of something forming slowly over time.

Q22.
Give a score of 0, 1, or 2 based on how many relevant details from the caption are given.
- Possible answers include that the canyon took millions of years to form, that water wore the rock away a little at a time, or that the canyon is now thousands of feet deep.

Q29.
Give a score of 0, 1, or 2 based on how many correct areas are given.
- The areas covered may include keeping fit and healthy, keeping active, reading and speaking, learning math, or learning English skills.

Q30.
Give a score of 0, 1, or 2 based on how well the answer meets the criteria listed below.
- It should identify the main purpose as being to describe some of the activities, to give examples of what the child will do, or to make the activities sound fun and/or useful.
- It should use relevant details from the passage.

Q33.
Give a score of 0, 1, or 2 based on how many acceptable reasons are given.
- Possible reasons listed could include that children under the age of five learn fitness habits they will keep for life, learn quickly, take in information quickly, and develop skills easier.

Q34.
Give a score of 0, 1, 2, or 3 based on how well the answer meets the criteria listed below.
- It should describe at least three benefits to children of attending the Shining Light Day Center.
- The benefits described should be based on the information in the passage.
- It should use relevant details from the passage.

Practice Test 3, Session 2

Question	Answer	Language Arts Florida Standard
41	C	Determine the meaning of words and phrases as they are used in a text, distinguishing literal from nonliteral language.
42	B	Describe characters in a story (e.g., their traits, motivations, or feelings) and explain how their actions contribute to the sequence of events.
43	D	Describe characters in a story (e.g., their traits, motivations, or feelings) and explain how their actions contribute to the sequence of events.
44	See Below	Ask and answer questions to demonstrate understanding of a text, referring explicitly to the text as the basis for the answers.
45	A	Determine the meaning of words and phrases as they are used in a text, distinguishing literal from nonliteral language.
46	D	Distinguish their own point of view from that of the narrator or those of the characters.
47	B	Recount stories, including fables, folktales, and myths from diverse cultures; determine the central message, lesson, or moral and explain how it is conveyed through key details in the text.
48	C	Determine the meaning of words and phrases as they are used in a text, distinguishing literal from nonliteral language.
49	afraid brave	Describe characters in a story (e.g., their traits, motivations, or feelings) and explain how their actions contribute to the sequence of events.
50	See Below	Distinguish their own point of view from that of the narrator or those of the characters.
51	See Below	Recount stories; determine the central message, lesson, or moral and explain how it is conveyed through key details in the text.
52	D	Determine the meaning of general academic and domain-specific words and phrases in a text.
53	C	Describe the relationship between a series of historical events, scientific ideas or concepts, or steps in technical procedures in a text, using language that pertains to time, sequence, and cause/effect.
54	B	Determine the main idea of a text; recount the key details and explain how they support the main idea.
55	A	Determine the meaning of general academic and domain-specific words and phrases in a text.
56	C	Use text features and search tools (e.g., key words, sidebars, hyperlinks) to locate information relevant to a given topic efficiently.
57	B	Ask and answer questions to demonstrate understanding of a text, referring explicitly to the text as the basis for the answers.
58	B	Use information gained from illustrations and the words in a text to demonstrate understanding of the text.
59	"suggest a lower price"	Determine the meaning of general academic and domain-specific words and phrases in a text.
60	See Below	Use information gained from illustrations and the words in a text to demonstrate understanding of the text.
61	See Below	Describe the logical connection between particular sentences and paragraphs in a text (e.g., comparison, cause/effect, first/second/third in a sequence).
62	See Below	Distinguish their own point of view from that of the author of a text.
63	See Below	Describe the relationship between a series of historical events, scientific ideas or concepts, or steps in technical procedures in a text, using language that pertains to time, sequence, and cause/effect.
64	A	Demonstrate command of the conventions of standard English capitalization, punctuation, and spelling when writing.

65	saw	Demonstrate command of the conventions of standard English capitalization, punctuation, and spelling when writing.
66	D	Demonstrate command of the conventions of standard English grammar and usage when writing or speaking.
67	A	Demonstrate command of the conventions of standard English capitalization, punctuation, and spelling when writing.
68	A	Demonstrate command of the conventions of standard English grammar and usage when writing or speaking.
69	C	Demonstrate command of the conventions of standard English capitalization, punctuation, and spelling when writing.
70	B	Determine the main ideas and supporting details of a text read aloud or information presented in diverse media and formats, including visually, quantitatively, and orally.
71	A	Ask and answer questions about information from a speaker, offering appropriate elaboration and detail.
72	B	Ask and answer questions about information from a speaker, offering appropriate elaboration and detail.
73	A	Ask and answer questions about information from a speaker, offering appropriate elaboration and detail.
74	2, 1, 4, 3	Ask and answer questions about information from a speaker, offering appropriate elaboration and detail.
75	A	Determine the main ideas and supporting details of a text read aloud or information presented in diverse media and formats, including visually, quantitatively, and orally.

Q44.
Give a score of 0, 1, or 2 based on how many relevant details are listed. Possible answers are listed below.
- He is quiet as they drive into the city. / He gasps when he looks up at the tower. / His stomach turns over. / He says that he's not sure if he can do it. / He takes a deep breath as he steps through the entrance. / He holds his father's hand.

Q50.
Give a score of 0, 1, or 2 based on how well the answer meets the criteria listed below.
- It should make a reasonable inference about how Toby feels at the end of the passage.
- The inference could be that he feels proud of himself, unafraid, or relieved.
- It should use relevant details from the passage.

Q51.
Give a score of 0, 1, or 2 based on how well the answer meets the criteria listed below.
- It should identify Toby's problem as that he has a fear of heights.
- It should describe how Toby faces his fear by climbing to the top of the Eiffel Tower.
- It should use relevant details from the passage.

Q60.
Give a score of 0, 1, or 2 based on how many relevant examples are given.
- Any reasonable answer can be accepted as long as it relates the art to passage content.
- The answer could refer to the items shown, the price tags, or the hanging clothes.

Q61.
Give a score of 0.5 for each sentence correctly matched with its purpose. The correct matches are listed below.
- A yard sale is when you sell items in your front yard. → to tell what a yard sale is
- People have yard sales to get rid of unwanted items. → to give the main reason for having a yard sale
- It can also be a good way to make some extra money. → to give a second reason for having a yard sale
- Here are some tips on how to have a good yard sale. → to tell what the passage is about

Q62.
Give a score of 0, 1, or 2 based on how well the answer meets the criteria listed below.
- It should give a reasonable explanation of why asking other people to join in would be a good idea.
- The benefits may include having more items to sell, having help to run it, or making more money.

Q63.
Give a score of 0.5 for each item placed in the correct column. The correct matches are listed below.
- The Week Before Your Yard Sale → put up flyers, tell your friends, run a newspaper ad
- On the Day of Your Yard Sale → put balloons up, set up the tables, put a sign in your street

LISTENING PASSAGES

Listening Passages: Practice Test 1

Instructions: Read each passage. After reading the passage, have students answer the questions in the test book.

A Tasty Trick

My dad has always said that I have to eat vegetables for my body to stay healthy. I never used to like vegetables much. I didn't really like the taste. So Dad decided to try something new to make sure I would eat them.

He started putting vegetables in dishes like spaghetti or inside meat pies. That way, I didn't even know I was eating vegetables. The funny thing was that I actually liked the taste. Now I no longer avoid vegetables. I am happy to eat them however they are served.

Big Ben

Big Ben is one of the United Kingdom's most famous landmarks. It is located in the Palace of Westminster in London. Big Ben is the term given to refer to the great bell of the clock at the north end of the building. Over time, the nickname has been used to refer to the clock and the clock tower too.

Its building was completed in April 1858, and it celebrated its 150th anniversary in 2009. Even though it is over 150 years old, it still looks beautiful. It looks down on the city like it is keeping watch on the people. One unusual feature is that the clock has four faces, which allows the clock to be seen from every angle. It is actually the largest four-faced chiming clock in the world. It is also the third largest freestanding clock in the world.

Listening Passages: Practice Test 2

Instructions: Read each passage. After reading the passage, have students answer the questions in the test book.

The Astronomer

An astronomer used to go out at night to observe the stars. One evening, he was wandering around town with his eyes fixed on the sky. He suddenly tripped and fell into a well. He sat there and groaned about his sores and bruises and cried for help. He pummeled his fists against the well. He looked up and all he could see were the stars. The twinkling stars looked back down on him and laughed.

The astronomer's friend finally heard his cries and made his way over to the well. After hearing the astronomer's story of how he fell, he simply shook his head.

"Old friend, in striving to see into the heavens, you don't manage to see what is on the earth," the friend said.

View from the Moon

Many people believe that the Great Wall of China can be viewed from the Moon. This is actually incorrect. No manmade structures are visible from the Moon at all. Continents, oceans, and cloud cover can be seen. But structures like buildings and walls cannot be seen.

It is true that the Great Wall of China can be viewed from space. But so can many other structures. These include motorways, cities, landmarks, and even fields of crops.

Listening Passages: Practice Test 3

Instructions: Read each passage. After reading the passage, have students answer the questions in the test book.

The Dog and the River

A dog was crossing a river by walking across a log. He had a small but juicy piece of meat in his mouth. He walked slowly across the log, while being careful not to lose his balance. As he looked down, he saw his own reflection in the water. He mistook the reflection for another dog. As he stared at the dog, he realized that the piece of meat it was carrying was larger than his own. He immediately dropped his own piece of meat and attacked the other dog to get the larger piece.

As he barked at the dog, his piece of meat fell from his mouth and into the water below. His paw struck at his reflection, only to hit the water below. At that moment, he realized that the other dog was only his reflection. He stared sadly at his small piece of meat as it floated away.

Hillary Clinton

Hillary Clinton was born on October 26, 1947. She was the First Lady of the United States from 1993 to 2001, as the wife of President Bill Clinton. In 2001, she became a senator for the state of New York. She remained in this role until 2009. In January of 2009, she became the 67th United States Secretary of State, serving under President Barack Obama. Just prior to this, Clinton was also considered as a candidate to run for president. She remained as Secretary of State until February, 2013.

Made in the USA
Middletown, DE
08 November 2018